The Politics of Resentment

Institute for Research on Public Policy
Founded in 1972, the Institute for Research on Public Policy is an independent, national, nonprofit organization. IRPP seeks to improve public policy in Canada by generating research, providing insight, and sparking debate that will contribute to the public policy decision-making process and strengthen the quality of the public policy decisions made by Canadian governments, citizens, institutions, and organizations. IRPP's independence is assured by an endowment fund, to which federal and provincial governments and the private sector have contributed.

As part of its mission, IRPP seeks to disseminate the diverse views and perspectives found in different parts of the country. Recently, the Institute has published a collection of essays on the divergent perspectives in Quebec and the rest of Canada on pivotal events in Canadian history; and a paper by IRPP Senior Scholar Tom Courchene on Ontario's place in the North American economic and political community. In an effort to build bridges between Canada's two main language communities, IRPP has also published English translations of a collection of reports offering the Quebec perspective on the social union and of Alain Dubuc's series of editorials on the future of the Quebec nation (*Policy Options*, June 2000). In joining forces with UBC Press to publish Philip Resnick's *The Politics of Resentment: British Columbia Regionalism and Canadian Unity*, IRPP is seeking to provide Canadians with a greater understanding of the forces shaping the political agenda and regional identity in Canada's westernmost province.

Philip Resnick

The Politics of Resentment: British Columbia Regionalism and Canadian Unity

INSTITUTE FOR RESEARCH ON PUBLIC POLICY

INSTITUT DE RECHERCHE EN POLITIQUES PUBLIQUES

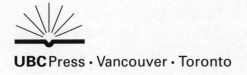

UBC Press · Vancouver · Toronto

An Institute for Research on Public Policy book published by UBC Press

Canadian Cataloguing in Publication Data

Resnick, Philip, 1944-
    The politics of resentment

    Includes bibliographical references and index.
    ISBN 0-7748-0804-7

    1. British Columbia – Politics and government. 2. Regionalism – Canada.
3. Federal-provincial relations – Canada – Public opinion.* 4. BC Unity Panel.
5. British Columbia – History – Autonomy and independence movements.*
6. Public opinion – British Columbia. I. Title.

FC3829.9.I5R47 2000   971.1′04   C00-910448-8
F1088.R47 2000

UBC Press acknowledges the financial support of the Government of Canada through the Book Publishing Industry Development Program (BPIDP) for our publishing activities.
Canadä

We also gratefully acknowledge the support of the Canada Council for the Arts for our publishing program, as well as the support of the British Columbia Arts Council.

Permissions Note:
Quotations on pages 5 and 59 are from "Pacific Door" and "David" from *The Collected Poems of Earle Birney*, Earle Birney © 1975. Used by written permission, McClelland & Stewart, Inc. *The Canadian Publishers*. Permission to quote from the Robin Skelton poem, "Night Poem, Vancouver Island" (on page 59) has been granted by the Skelton estate.

Set in Stone by Brenda and Neil West, BN Typographics West
Printed and bound in Canada by Friesens
Copy editor: Francis Chow
Proofreader: Deborah Kerr
Indexer: Heather Ebbs

UBC Press
University of British Columbia
2029 West Mall, Vancouver, BC V6T 1Z2
(604) 822-5959
Fax: (604) 822-6083
E-mail: info@ubcpress.ubc.ca
www.ubcpress.ubc.ca

For my family

Contents

Preface

I have had an interest in British Columbia politics ever since coming to this province in 1971. In my early years here, I was particularly interested in questions related to BC political economy. But I also began to follow the province's shifting political currents, from the New Democratic Party government of the early 1970s, to the restraint policies of the Social Credit government of the mid-1980s, to the realignment of provincial politics in the 1990s.

Like many others who have made BC their home, I felt that this province was different. The politics was a good deal zanier than in Ontario, where I had spent a number of years as a graduate student in the late 1960s and early 1970s. Nor did it resemble that of my native Quebec, where, coming of political age during the Quiet Revolution, I had experienced the politics of the new nationalism firsthand.

Out here on the Pacific Coast, Ottawa seemed far away and federal issues seemed to matter less than in places further east. BC's political divisions between right and left seemed to be cast in concrete, with business and its supporters and trade unions and their supporters squaring off against one another with passionate intensity. Social movements such as environmentalism, the peace movement, and New Age religions cropped up like magic mushrooms in the rain. For its part, the BC media, with an eye for the larger-than-life scandals that periodically rocked the province, treated what passed for politics as a blood sport.

To be honest, I found – and still find – the minutiae of BC politics of little interest. My horizons are more Canadian than British Columbian; more global, for that matter, than purely national. I suspect I am not the only British Columbian to feel this way. At the same time, I have found myself drawn over the past decade or so into the Canadian unity debate, which is primarily a debate about Quebec's place in

Confederation. I have had occasion to participate in this debate in various ways – briefs to parliamentary committees, conference papers, a regular column between 1995 and 1997 in the Montreal newspaper *Le Devoir,* and the writing of a number of book-length essays: *Letters to a Québécois Friend* (1990), *Toward a Canada-Quebec Union* (1991), and *Thinking English Canada* (1994).

I sometimes thought of undertaking a book-length study on British Columbia. Invariably something else intervened, and my attention shifted elsewhere. Yet the desire to come to terms with the province that I had come to call home never quite left me. Finally, a series of events in 1997 led me to return to the study of BC via the debate about Canadian unity.

That autumn, Victor Armony, a recent PhD graduate from the Université du Québec à Montréal (UQAM), came to work with me at the University of British Columbia as a postdoctoral student. Victor's doctoral thesis had involved the study of political discourse in his native Argentina, and he had also been part of a research project at UQAM involving the computerized textual analysis of documents.

We decided to embark on a comparative study of BC regionalism and Quebec nationalism. We hoped to combine the analytical, narrative approach that I have brought to much of my work with the computerized textual analysis that Victor had adopted. I approached the BC Intergovernmental Relations Secretariat for help in obtaining copies of speeches that had been made by BC premiers and intergovernmental affairs ministers, principally to federal-provincial conferences, and they obliged with some thirty or so documents. Doug McArthur, then deputy minister to the premier, was particularly helpful in expediting my request, and I thank him for it. These official documents form the backbone of Chapter 2.

Subsequently, the editor of the *Vancouver Sun,* John Cruickshank, and the *Sun* librarian, Debbie Millward, provided access to *Sun* files dealing with Canadian unity from the 1970s through the 1990s. I thank them both for their help. No small number of quotations, particularly in Chapters 2 and 3, come from this source.

Finally, during the autumn of 1997, the BC government, in the aftermath of the Calgary Declaration, set up the BC Unity Panel to tour the province and garner the opinions of British Columbians on issues related to Canadian unity. When the panel's report was released in February 1998, we were given access to the official transcripts of all the public hearings as well as to the written briefs that had been submitted to the panel. This material forms the basis for Chapter 4.

By the spring of 1998, it became clear that we had gathered a good deal of material on British Columbia – so much, in fact, that it made sense to drop the Quebec component of the study and to focus on BC exclusively. The goal became to produce a book on BC and Canadian unity.

When Victor Armony joined the Department of Sociology at the University of Ottawa later that year, he was no longer able to participate in the project as one of the co-authors. He has, however, made a direct contribution to this book: the second section of Chapter 4 is his undertaking. He has also contributed a good deal, through discussions and exchanges, to the project, and I thank him very warmly for this.

So in 1999, I finally found myself tackling the book on British Columbia that I had always managed to put off. It deals with the theme of BC regionalism and Canadian unity. Implicitly, however, it aims at something more. It represents my attempt to explore what makes BC stand apart as a region of Canada. It provides an analysis – the first, I think, that has ever been attempted in book-length format – of the reactions of the inhabitants of Canada's westernmost province to the challenges posed by Quebec nationalism, reactions often characterized by resentment. And it represents my attempt to provide a new formulation for describing BC's place within the Canadian federation.

Chapter 1 is an overview of some of the things that historians, social scientists, writers, and politicians have had to say, over the years, about this most particular province. It is also an attempt to come to terms with some of the theoretical literature that explores the theme of regionalism. In that sense, it is meant to set the stage for what follows.

Chapter 2 involves a close examination of the views of BC premiers from W.A.C. Bennett to Glen Clark and of other leading BC politicians on a number of questions. These include attitudes towards Quebec, attitudes towards the federal government and federal institutions, views on BC as a distinct region, attitudes towards BC separatism, and, finally, visions of Canada.

Chapter 3 looks at the same five themes discussed in Chapter 2, but examines them from the point of view of a broad range of BC opinion-makers: business spokespersons, trade union representatives, consultants, journalists, academics, ex-politicians, environmentalists, and others.

Chapter 4 looks closely at the proceedings of the BC Unity Panel in the autumn of 1997. The first section summarizes some of the findings of an extensive poll that was undertaken for the Unity Panel. The second section involves computerized textual analysis of the submissions to the public hearings of the Unity Panel. The third section involves a detailed analysis of some of the written briefs submitted to the Unity Panel. Both the second and third sections explore the same five themes as Chapters 2 and 3.

Chapter 5 tries to think more globally about the implications of the material presented in Chapters 1 to 4. It rejects the notion of region-state that has been promoted by a number of recent commentators. Instead, it proposes a new way of looking at Canada, in which BC would find its symbolic place as one of Canada's region-provinces.

Finally, Chapter 6 represents a short excursus into the business of future-gazing. What if Quebec were to vote "yes" in a third referendum on sovereignty? How would British Columbians be likely to react? What might their role be in keeping a post-Quebec Canada together?

In addition to those I have already thanked above, let me mention a few others:

- the University of British Columbia, which, through its Hampton Funds, provided the author with a grant to help in researching this book
- Verne Macdonnell, then a fourth-year undergraduate student at UBC, for his able research help during the 1998-99 academic year
- Donald Blake, Department of Political Science, UBC, and Allan Smith, Department of History, UBC, who read the opening chapter of this book and provided valuable feedback
- the two anonymous readers for UBC Press, as well as Paul Howe, Research Director, Politics, of the Institute for Research in Public Policy in Montreal, and Emily Andrew, editor at UBC Press, for insightful comments and suggestions
- the Société Québécoise de Science Politique and the Canadian Political Science Association, which provided venues in May and June 1999 where I could present versions of Chapters 1 and 2.

Philip Resnick
Vancouver, 1999

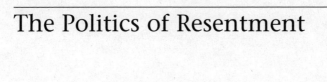

The Politics of Resentment

1
British Columbia as a Distinct Region of Canada

What accounts for some of British Columbia's peculiarities as a province of Canada? What are some of the ways in which social scientists have defined regionalism, and how might one fruitfully compare and contrast regionalism with nationalism? How has BC regionalism in recent decades been influenced by the development of Quebec nationalism and by the ongoing debate about Canadian unity? These are some of the questions that this opening chapter explores.

British Columbia has been a province of Canada since 1871, but it has always been an awkward partner in Confederation. From the very beginning, its political leaders threatened to go their own way if Ottawa failed to live up to the terms of its agreement to build a railway to the Pacific within ten years. "I would not object to a little revolution now and again in British Columbia, after Confederation, if we were treated unfairly; for I am one of those who believe that political hatreds attest the vitality of the state," argued Amor de Cosmos, one of BC's early premiers.[1] In 1876, the BC legislature, unhappy with delays in the construction of the transcontinental railway, passed a motion threatening secession from Canada.[2] Not for nothing did John A. Macdonald come to describe British Columbia as "the spoilt child of the dominion."[3]

The first Conservative premier of the province, Richard McBride, fought the Laurier government tooth and claw over the amount of federal subsidies to BC. When he walked out of a 1906 federal-provincial conference in protest over what he took to be BC's inequitable treatment, he was received as a conquering hero back home; approving crowds greeted his train from Revelstoke on, and band music and a banquet were laid out in his honour when he arrived in Victoria.[4]

Successive provincial governments have played the anti-Ottawa card over and over again. Duff Pattullo did so in the 1930s, first over the high cost of social expenditures for the unemployed, then over the recommendations of the Rowell-Sirois Royal Commission report in the late 1930s that greater powers be given to the federal government. "We who are beyond the Rocky Mountains want to be left free to act ... we do not want to be hogtied and hamstrung, and that is exactly what will happen if this report is implemented."[5] W.A.C. Bennett wrapped himself in the flag of defender of provincial interests when it came to the development of electricity on both the Columbia and Peace Rivers, picking fights with the federal government and powerful Vancouver-based economic interests, and winning: "We had an empire to build. There were various projects to the south, more to the north, while further north was the Yukon and Alaska ... Very important this Canada North. It had to be developed."[6] Glen Clark attempted to mobilize regionalist sentiments in the summer of 1996, taking on the federal government in his defence of BC fishermen caught up in a dispute with their Alaskan counterparts over diminishing salmon stocks: "British Columbia is going to have to demand more jurisdiction over fisheries. We just cannot rely on the federal government ... They just don't understand British Columbia."[7]

The sense of being a geographical region apart seems deeply ingrained in the BC psyche. BC's harsh climate caught the attention of early travellers and settlers. "New Caledonia (north and west of the Columbia region)," wrote the American historian Robert Greenhow in 1845, "is a sterile land of snow-clad mountains, tortuous rivers and lakes frozen over nearly 2/3 of the year; presenting scarcely a spot in which any of the vegetables used as a food by civilized people can be produced."[8] John McLean recounted his experience at the Hudson's Bay Company post in Fort George in the mid-nineteenth century in these words: "The situation of the post is exceedingly dreary, standing on the right bank of Fraser's River, having in front a high hill that shades the sun until late morning, and in the midst of a 'woods and wilds, whose melancholy gloom' is maddening enough."[9] A disappointed speculator wrote in 1862 that in BC "the impressions left on the mind are of grandeur, gloomy vastness, awful solitude, rendered more dismal by the howl of the beasts of prey."[10]

The mood would change to something more positive in the twentieth century, as Maria Tippett and Douglas Cole have noted with particular reference to BC artists: "By the 1940s British Columbians and their artists had accepted the land. Wilderness or cultivated, the landscape had become part of them. No longer exotic or alien, it was here and it was home. The conifer retained its dark solemnity, but it was no longer gloomy. The coastal waters retained their awesomeness, but they were no longer fearsome or foreign."[11]

Yet a sense of distance from known places and of the overwhelming presence of nature still dominated reflections. "Geographically, BC was far removed from the seat of [Federal] Government. An almost insuperable barrier of mountains cut it off from the rest of the British possessions. The country ... was in every sense foreign to Canada," wrote R.E. Gosnell, the province's first librarian and archivist, in 1913.[12] "All night the demon monster has been rushing us into the West," wrote Emily Carr of a train trip back to her native province. "It is the West now, no trace of East left – low sky, dense growth, cruel rivers, power and intensity everywhere."[13] Earle Birney, in one of his many poems celebrating British Columbia, observed:

Drake's crewmen scribbled here their paradise
And dying Baring lost in fog
Turned north to mark us off from Asia still.
Here cool Cook traced in sudden blood his final bay
And scurvied traders trailed the wakes of yesterday
Until the otter rocks were bare
And all the tribal feathers blackened.
Here Spaniards and Vancouver's boatsmen scrawled
The problem that is ours and yours
That there is no clear Strait of Arain
To lead us easy back to Europe.[14]

And Robin Skelton noted: "In BC there is no place free from [nature's] presence. Vancouver, an immensely modern city, can never become a wholly urban environment, for it is pinned down between the mountains and the sea, and the mountains are always visible and the sea is always near ... Thus, even the most urban of BC poets cannot avoid themes and images of the wilderness."[15]

For their part, the economic foundations of the province did not rest on a single commodity such as wheat, as was the case for the Prairie provinces. Fur, fish, minerals, and lumber all played a role. The result, as Thomas Sanford argued, was that "BC has been more of a 'company province,' dotted by company-owned or company-based towns and organized by large enterprises."[16] BC's resource-based economy, moreover, was less of a beneficiary of the National Policy than was central Canada's. "BC bears an unduly large share in the support of Confederation ... It is estimated that approximately 80% of the manufacturing commodities imported into BC are imported from eastern Canada, while approximately 75% of our main primary products, apart from agriculture, are sold in open competition in the world's markets ... BC buys in a protected market and sells in an unprotected one," was the complaint from British Columbia in the province's brief to the Rowell-Sirois Royal Commission in 1938.[17]

In the years following the Second World War, exports to Britain declined drastically while those to the United States increased, coming to constitute approximately 50 percent of all BC exports by the early 1980s.[18] This helps explain the strong support from both BC business and the BC government for the Canada–United States Free Trade Agreement.[19] Over the past couple of decades, however, there has also been a pronounced shift in British Columbia trade to the Asia-Pacific region. In 1996, for example, 35 percent of BC's exports went to Asia; in comparison, only 9 percent of overall Canadian exports went to that part of the world.[20]

Politically, the British tradition dominated for the first seventy-five years, embedded in the very name of the province. On a per capita basis, recruitment rates from British Columbia into the Canadian armed forces during both the First and Second World Wars were the highest in Canada.[21] Margaret Ormsby saw British Columbia as "a British community whose provincialism is rooted in the large cosmopolitan civilization of a world-wide empire."[22] Walter Sage, writing in 1937, could describe the province as "distinctly British."[23]

The period after the Second World War – an era of growing continentalism in the economic, cultural, and political spheres, saw an increased American orientation in British Columbia, much as in the rest of Canada.[24] It also saw an increasing diversity in the ethnic makeup of the population. Much of this reflected postwar immigration from continental Europe. By 1961, for example, people of German background, who had made up only 2.7 percent of the province in 1941, constituted 7.2 percent of the total; those of Scandinavian background, 5.9 percent; and those of French background, 4 percent.[25]

Over the past two decades, there has been a further shift – this time from Europe to Asia. With immigration into British Columbia in the 1980s and early 1990s averaging 30,000 a year, and with 80 percent of the new migrants being of Asian (e.g., Hong Kong, Taiwan, China, Philippines, India) origin, the ethnic makeup of the province has further changed.[26] The 1991 census, for example, showed 5.6 percent of

BC's population as Chinese in origin, 3.2 percent as East Indian, and 2.5 percent of other Asian origins; in the Vancouver school system in 1995, English was the primary language of the home for 44 percent of the students, followed by Chinese for 31 percent, Vietnamese for 5 percent, and Punjabi for 4 percent.[27] The British Columbia of today bears only a distant relationship to the essentially British outpost of settlement of the late nineteenth or early twentieth century.

In its origins, the political culture of British Columbia was marked by a non-party tradition. When political parties were established in the early twentieth century, there was relatively little to distinguish the Conservatives from the Liberals. It was only with the coming of the Co-operative Commonwealth Federation (CCF) in the 1930s that things began to change. The provincial political system came to be defined along an anti-socialist versus socialist spectrum. A Liberal-Conservative coalition held power between 1941 and 1952. This was followed by the rise of Social Credit, which dominated the provincial political landscape between 1952 and 1972 and again between 1975 and 1991. The result was a provincial party system quite unlike that which existed at the federal level or which could be found in most other Canadian provinces. As Alan Cairns observed: "The divergence of federal and provincial party systems in British Columbia was neither accidental nor inevitable ... The free enterprise versus socialism dichotomy brandished by W.A.C. Bennett ... the reception and success of the same strategy by the new Social Credit party of Bill Bennett is testament to powerful strains in the political culture of provincial politics."[28] David Elkins has argued that "British Columbia operates two distinct party systems. It is isolated from Canada – and many people are proud of that – but steadfastly attached to Canada – and they are proud of that too."[29] It is notable that even today a provincial party like the BC Liberals retains considerable distance from its federal namesake, having a completely separate organization.

It is also worth noting that BC voters were not given to voting for the winning party at the federal level during the Pearson and Trudeau period, and that in the 1990s the Reform Party, outside of its home base of Alberta, has been most successful in electing members of Parliament in British Columbia – twenty-four in the 1993 federal election and twenty-five in 1997. BC is a region whose inhabitants seem comfortable in the role of outsiders vis-à-vis the federal government, although they will complain vociferously about being ignored and rise up in fury against the federal government when a contentious issue arises. The views of longtime letters-to-the-editor writer Harry Pick are typical: "Western Canada is no closer to Ontario and Quebec than it was 77 years ago."[30]

The political polarization of the province between right and left (or, more correctly, between centre-right and centre-left) is reflected in underlying social traditions. On the one hand, there has been a strongly individualistic streak, reflected in early resource entrepreneurs such as Robert Dunsmuir and the so-called robber barons and in a hard-line defence of law and order against radical unionists at the turn of the century or in the crisis conditions of the 1930s. Thus Vancouver mayor Gerry McGeer could read the riot act against labour activists in 1935, seeing his city as "being victimized by an organized conspiracy to capitalize, for revolutionary purposes, [on] the conditions of depression which now exist."[31] Bruce Hutchison, the veteran *Vancouver Sun* journalist, described Vancouver's economic elite in the period immediately following the Second World War in the following terms: "Vancouver is ruled by the most garish tycoons produced to date in Canada. The capitalists who draw dividends, the entrepreneurs who live in luxury on the toil of countless unknown men in the wilderness, the financiers and promoters of sudden eminence form a distinct caste as in every entrepot of commerce. Here they are rather bolder and much franker in their ambition than the same caste in the East."[32] And Edwin Black wrote: "An extreme orientation towards action is typical of frontier communities – as is the lack of respect for traditional political procedures ... Because traditional procedures are restraints, action-oriented politicians have little interest in them, and neither do their constituents ... His tactics, in Mr. Bennett's own idiom, represented 'Progress-not-politics.'"[33]

Some of the same rough-and-tumble values were reflected in fairly belligerent positions taken by municipal and provincial politicians on the right against the counterculture in the 1960s, or in the neo-conservative restraint measures brought in by the Social Credit government in the 1980s during a period of economic downturn, in a double-barrelled assault against public sector expenditures and public sector unions.[34] BC, it is also worth noting, is home to Canada's financially best-endowed think tank, the Fraser Institute, known for its unflinching defence of free market principles.

On the other side of the spectrum, there has been a utopian/radical streak to the province, associated with more egalitarian values. At the turn of the twentieth century, some of the early socialists in British Columbia came to be known as "impossiblists," so unyielding was their vision of the necessity of an immediate transformation of capitalism. It was in BC that the Wobblies (Industrial Workers of the World) found significant support in logging camps and mining towns in the 1900s; that strong anti-war sentiment came to be expressed by labour leaders like Ginger Goodwin in 1917-18; that movements to organize the unemployed and to march on Ottawa came into existence during the "Dirty Thirties."[35]

BC was the seeding ground for utopian experiments, with Finnish fishing villages based on cooperative principles, such as Sointula, flourishing off Vancouver Island and Doukhobour settlements harbouring Tolstoyan-pacifist refugees from tsarist Russia taking root in the Kootenays. In more recent decades, BC was the home of Canada's most radical student movement, at Simon Fraser University in the 1960s; the scene of a general public sector strike in the mid-1980s and of Canada's largest peace marches; the place where international environmental movements such as Greenpeace were born and where major battles against clearcutting were waged in the 1990s at Clayoquot Sound;[36] the scene of the most divisive university battles in Canada around questions of political correctness;[37] and the venue for a major anti-APEC (Asia-Pacific Economic Cooperation) demonstration at the University of British Columbia in November 1997 whose repercussions would be felt for several years in police commission inquiries and political controversy.

"Right-wing bigots" and "left-wing zealots," as they have sometimes been termed (or, to use more dispassionate, scholarly language, people with strong views, both on the right and left), have seemed equally at home in British Columbia. The pervasive centre, so characteristic a feature of Canadian politics at the federal level, has not always found a happy camping ground in the polarized politics of the province.

Another important feature of BC society is a proclivity towards fluid, shifting values. The province has experienced continuous population growth throughout its history. In 1871, when BC entered Confederation, its population accounted for a bare 1 percent of the Canadian total. This rose to 2 percent in 1891, 5.5 percent in 1911, 6.5 percent in 1931, and 9 percent by 1961.[38] By 1996, BC's share of Canada's population had grown to 13 percent; between 1991 and 1996, the rate of growth of its population was more than twice the Canadian average.[39] Not only have outsiders continuously migrated to the province from abroad; interprovincial migration has also benefited BC through much of the twentieth century, with significant population inflow from the Prairies, Ontario, Quebec, and the Maritimes.[40]

All of these have implications for political culture. A December 1998 survey of the Greater Vancouver area found that 58 percent of respondents had been born outside BC.[41] As Gordon Galbraith noted in the 1970s: "British Columbia has always been populated principally by people who came from elsewhere ... In 1971, only 48% of the population were born in British Columbia; by way of contrast, 68% of the population of Ontario were born in that province ... Because the electorate comes from diverse historical backgrounds and lacks a common heritage, political appeals to the past, to historical symbols, are limited or absent, and political rhetoric tends to revolve around the future."[42] A decade earlier, Cyril Belshaw had pointedly challenged the very existence of any shared BC values: "There has been the assumption that the province exists, the Province of British Columbia. Now I wonder whether it does truly exist in anything but the political sense ... In what sense are we really in British Columbia a society?"[43]

Certain characteristics of contemporary BC do stand out, however. It is the region of North America with the highest percentage of people without any religious affiliation whatsoever – 37 percent, according to a 1996 survey.[44] Or, to place it in the Canadian context, it is a province where only 42 percent of the inhabitants consider religion to be an important part of their lives, compared with 60 percent of Canadians as a whole.[45] It is nonetheless home both to fundamentalist denominations of Christianity and to New Age religions. The secular versus religious divide is reflected in the much greater support shown by those who define themselves as secularists than by those who define themselves as evangelical Christians for abortion or gay rights,[46] and by the polarization on such questions as access to abortion during the premiership of Bill Vander Zalm or the availability of gay-related library materials in Surrey schools in 1997-98.

BC has high rates of divorce,[47] drug use,[48] and crime compared with the Canadian average: "For property crimes, BC continues to report a much higher rate than the other provinces ... Consistent with previous years, the crime rate [for the nine largest Canadian metropolitan areas] continues to be highest in Vancouver."[49] As Thomas Sanford argued back in 1961: "The greater the deviance in one sphere, the more likely the deviance in other spheres ... In the BC case today, we see a deviant province with the highest rates of alcoholism, addiction, accidents, delinquency, strikes and suicides to be found in Canada. Generally, deviance from traditional institutions and traditional patterns of action are fertile grounds for protest parties."[50]

Traditional values have less of a hold in British Columbia than older, settled regions of Canada. As BC writer Brian Fawcett describes it, "Part of it is that crazy Jack Kerouac thing. It's the end of the world."[51]

Yet deviance (or flakiness, if one prefers that term) in certain areas may be combined with a high degree of seriousness in others. Stephen Bengston of Viewpoints Research notes a strong concern in both native and adoptive Vancouverites for the environment, for education, and for hard work, values that are making for a distinct Vancouver culture. "With the possible exception of Torontonians, we are probably the most intense of all Canadians."[52]

This brings us to the larger question of the definition of region. Region is hardly a new construct in the social sciences. In the 1930s, Lewis Mumford wrote: "Between the continent and the historic village is an area sometimes larger, sometimes smaller than a political state. It is the human region."[53] In a study of American regionalism from the same period, Howard Odum and Harry Moore argued: "A key attribute of the region is that it must be a *constituent unit in an aggregate whole or totality.*"[54] For its part, the European Union, in a 1997 document published by its Committee of Regions, argues: "A region is a politico-territorial unit built directly below the national level with its own government and autonomous powers."[55] And Michael Keating, in a recent study, defines region "as an intermediate level between the state and the locality."[56]

According to these definitions, the region is something encompassed within a larger nation-state. As in the case of the nation-state, however, there are geographical, economic, political, and cultural factors at work in the concept of region. Canada, it has been argued, is at a deeper symbolic level "very much a country of regions, of what have been called 'limited identities.'"[57] As Robert Kroetsch notes: "Where the impulse in the United States is usually to define oneself as American, the Canadian ... is always quoting his many sources. Our sense of region resists our national sense. I hear myself saying I'm from Western Canada."[58] For Michael Ornstein, "the people of different regions exhibit regional loyalties, in the sense of preferring the quality of life of their province and/or supporting their province's claims against the federal government."[59]

Canada's federal structure reinforces this sense of regionalism, giving to its provinces substantial powers over economic resources, social policy, and local affairs. In the absence of strong cabinet ministers from BC at the federal level – as has often been the case over the past forty years – a distinctly provincial political culture has been rein-forced. As Donald Smiley observed in the late 1970s, "the Pearson-Trudeau Liberals have governed Canada without providing an effective outlet in the party for attitudes and interests which are specifically western. The circumstance confers on the provincial leaders an almost exclusive franchise to represent these interests and contributes pow-erfully to other provincialist influences."[60] Alan Cairns has argued, in an equally institutionalist vein, "support for powerful, independent provincial governments is a product of the political system itself ... fostered and created by provincial government elites employing the policy-making apparatus of their jurisdictions."[61]

Is BC regionalism, then, a constructed identity, in the way that some theorists of nationalism talk about the invention of tradition or imagined national communities?[62] Or do BC's inhabitants have a regional outlook, grounded in certain objective realities? For long, BC could be seen as "a colony within a colony."[63] As it has come of age, however, a growing sense of living apart has come to influence the way in which its inhabitants think about the larger country to which they belong. As a resource-rich periphery, BC has over the decades prospered from its forest, mineral, and fishing wealth. Ever since fig-ures became available in 1926, the province has invariably been ranked among the leading provinces in terms of per capita income.[64] The position of BC within Canada is very much that of a "have" rather than a "have-not" province.

In the era of globalization now upon us, regionalism has gained a whole new lease on life. Regions have begun to acquire greater impor-tance in Europe, crossing national lines and transforming the mech-anism for making and implementing public policy.[65] Kenichi Ohmae has talked about the international emergence of the region-state: "The glue holding traditional nation states together, at least in eco-nomic terms, has begun to dissolve ... By contrast, the territorial divid-ing lines that do make sense belong to what I call 'region states' – geographical units like northern Italy, Baden-Würtemberg, the Silicon Valley/Bay Area, etc. ... In a borderless world, these are the natural economic zones."[66]

Ohmae has his Canadian counterparts. Thomas Courchene, for example, suggests "that Ontario's shift from heartland to region eco-nomic state is more or less inevitable and its implications strike at the very heart of Canadian federalism and indeed Canada. This is every bit as much a national challenge as it is an Ontario challenge, especially since similar pressures are driving British Columbia and

Quebec ... Intergovernmentalism will become more important and more pervasive."[67] And David Wolfe notes: "Evidence is accumulating that changes occurring at the regional level are every bit as significant as those at the supra-national level. Regional economies consist of more than just individual behaviours or firms, or even networks of firms, and their employees. They are also constituted by the cultural traditions and institutional structures that facilitate and regulate economic behaviour and social activity."[68]

Where British Columbia is concerned, Norman Ruff has observed: "Global economic change has renewed the sense of a Pacific distinctiveness from the Prairie neighbours beyond the Rockies, and has combined with national political changes to breed a determination to give an overriding priority to British Columbia's own agenda."[69] This makes it easier for political figures like Gordon Wilson to argue a BC-first position: "By virtue of the natural valley corridors that run north/south, British Columbia has ready access to the American markets to its south ... Well situated on the Pacific Rim, it has excellent potential for expanded trade with the rapidly developing economies of [Asia] ... In short, we have a solid economy upon which to build a satisfying, comfortable, *limits-to-growth* future appropriate to the demands and limitations of the 21st century."[70]

BC's locational position also underlines the stance taken by commentators like Gordon Gibson: "The provinces of the West, especially Alberta and British Columbia, have gained a maturity and strength that leaves them chafing at the old relationship with Ottawa."[71] And it underlines the call of a writer like George Woodcock for "regions conscious of their own identity ... overleap[ing] the limitations of nationality and tak[ing] their own places in the broader world."[72]

One needs to be careful, however. Regionalism, like nationalism, a force to which it can fruitfully be compared, can have its ups and downs. It can take open or closed forms. It can speak to legitimate concerns that the inhabitants of a particular geographical space have about their society or province, but it can also take on an aura of chauvinism and disdain towards other regions, or towards the larger nation-state to which a particular region belongs. Moreover, regionalism is linked to questions of identity, which in the world in which we live can take multiple forms.

Michael Keating observes: "Political identities are complex and increasingly multiple, but do tend to be linked to territory, a place, a homeland. Territory is the principal basis for political mobilization, because of its link to identity and for purely practical reasons. It is also the main foundation for political representation and account-ability."[73] As the prevailing definitions of regionalism would suggest, the inhabitants of regions see themselves as members of a larger component unit; therefore, territories and identities are seldom seen as exclusive. There is a local or regional tropism at work, but there is also the pull of the larger nation, especially in periods of crisis such as economic depression, war, or the threat of potential breakup. There is the possibility of cyclical downturns as well as upturns in an export-oriented economy like BC's. There are nationalizing, as well as region-alizing, cultural factors at work where the sense of political identity is concerned.

Henry Crease, BC's attorney general, made the following observation in supporting the case for British Columbia's entry into Confedera-tion during the 1870 debate on the question: "We are sandwiched between the US territory to the north and south – indeed on all sides but one, and that one opening toward Canada. Our only option is between remaining a petty, isolated community, 15,000 miles from home, eking out a miserable existence on the crumbs of prosperity our powerful and active Republican neighbours choose to allow us, or, by taking our place among the comity of nations, become the western outlet on the North Pacific of a young and vigorous people."[74]

Have BC's geopolitical options – the British imperial one aside – really changed all that much, even with a population of 4 million today? Louis Wirth, a distinguished American sociologist, offered the following critique of the limitations of regionalism fifty years ago: "As a counterpoise to gigantism, to uniformity, to standardization, and to overcentralization, regionalism can have wholesome effects; but these legitimate aspirations can also degenerate into regional cultism and jingoism and lend themselves to exploitation by political and cultural demagogues."[75] We need to bear this in mind when confronted with the arguments of Ohmae or Courchene.

Rich regions can all too easily become resentful of poorer ones. One sees this at work in recent years with the Lega Nord in northern Italy seeking autonomy, even independence, from Rome; or in Belgium, where the Flemish region is increasingly resentful of the Walloon one, for example, when it comes to social security expenditures.[76] The leader of the Flemish region has proclaimed: "In all countries in Europe – Italy, Spain, the United Kingdom – people understand the necessity of devolving power to regional entities."[77] Michael Keating notes: "Wealthy regions which are not politically dominant are likely to be decentralist, as in Lombardy and Catalonia."[78]

There are hints of the same tensions at work in the rich province versus poor province syndrome that sometimes colours BC views of Canadian federalism and of the powers of the federal government. W.A.C. Bennett could characterize BC "as a goblet to be drained"[79] and attack federal equalization payments to the poorer provinces as a raid on the BC treasury.[80] Bill Vander Zalm could support the Meech Lake Accord because he saw it as a means to decentralize federal power and break southern Ontario's hold over national economic policy.[81] A New Democratic Party government in the mid-1990s could attempt to impose a three-month waiting period on welfare recipients from other parts of Canada who moved to the province, even though its actions triggered cuts in transfer payments from Ottawa under the Canada Assistance Plan.

Regionalism also gained considerable importance in BC over the past four decades, as a new Quebec nationalism entered on the scene. What began with the Quiet Revolution of the 1960s led to the first election of a Parti Québécois government in Quebec in 1976 and to referenda on sovereignty in 1980 and 1995. It also resulted in constitutional debates, beginning with the Victoria Charter of 1971 and continuing through the patriation of the constitution in 1982, the Meech Lake Accord of the late 1980s, the Charlottetown Accord and Canada-wide referendum of 1992, and the Calgary Declaration of 1997.

These developments constitute the backdrop for the study contained in this book. I will be looking at the reactions in British Columbia to the Quebec-generated challenge to the future of the Canadian federation. With Quebec political leaders and Quebec public opinion speaking the language of Quebec nationalism, how would British Columbians come to define their own province and region? Is there a peculiarly British Columbian take on the national unity question? Would a greater sense of British Columbia as a community able to follow its own destiny take hold in reaction to continuous Quebec discontent and the growing possibility that Canada might not in the end survive as a federation that includes Quebec?

At a minimum, the Quebec question could lead to a vigorous reaffirmation of the view of BC as a distinct region of Canada. The origins of such a position can be traced back to an earlier period. The historian Walter Sage, writing between the wars, noted: "The isolation of the province from the rest of Canada is an essential fact. British Columbians are Canadians with a difference."[82] Following the Second World War, civil servants and geographers began to commonly divide Canada into five regions.[83] But it was Premier W.A.C. Bennett, at a federal-provincial conference in the late 1960s, who really put the cat among the pigeons with his call for a five-region Canada to replace the ten-province Canada we know. (Bennett's scheme would have seen the Yukon thrown in with BC for good measure!)[84] And it was his son, Bill Bennett, premier from 1975 to 1986, who carried on the crusade with his 1978 call for transforming the Senate into a sort of House of the Provinces, to better "take account of important regional needs and aspirations, including those of British Columbia."[85]

Just how seriously all this was meant is open to speculation. But it certainly bespoke the desire of key BC political actors, and sections of public opinion in the province, to secure recognition for BC's distinctiveness vis-à-vis the other provinces and the federal government. The reaction of BC politicians to Quebec's growing nationalist demands reflected something of the same spirit. Bill Vander Zalm, at the time Quebec's distinctiveness was being discussed during the Meech Lake round, proposed that the constitution recognize the uniqueness of British Columbia and all other provinces no less than that of Quebec.[86] In introducing the Calgary Declaration for ratification in the BC legislature in 1998, intergovernmental affairs minister Andrew Petter declared that "British Columbians have a keen sense of our own identity, and of the things that distinguish us from the rest of the country."[87]

There were different ways in which British Columbians could affirm their distinctiveness. In the 1960s, W.A.C. Bennett, an archfoe of the federal government where the Columbia River Treaty had been concerned, wrapped himself in the old imperial flag in staking out a position on the national unity question. "As your premier and political leader I say that if the rest of Canada breaks up and goes elsewhere, BC will always remain an integral part of the great British Commonwealth of Nations. To me the Union Jack is the greatest flag and always will be."[88] There was strong opposition in BC to special status for Quebec, stronger than in almost any other part of Canada. This found expression in anti-Quebec sentiment in the run-up to the Meech Lake Accord;[89] and in the 68 percent "no" vote in BC in the October 1992 referendum on the Charlottetown Accord.[90] (Also worth noting with regard to BC political sentiments during this period is support in excess of 80 percent for referenda and for the recall of elected representatives expressed by BC voters in separate balloting on these questions during the November 1991 provincial election.) In the aftermath of the second Quebec referendum on sovereignty, there were calls by 1997 for British Columbia to go it alone if Quebec were to leave Canada:

"Independent BC viable, ex-Liberal chief claims";[91] "Angry Carney says BC shouldn't rule out separation";[92] "The senator struck a nerve in BC";[93] "25% of BC residents back separation."[94]

Such views, however, need to be balanced against evidence of overwhelming support within British Columbia for both Canadian unity and the Canadian identity. Although some observers have been tempted to think of BC as constituting a "nation within a nation,"[95] close to 90 percent of British Columbia respondents who are surveyed think of Canada, not of British Columbia, as constituting their nation.[96] In Quebec, by contrast, support for remaining a province of Canada hovers around 61 percent, while close to one-third of respondents want Quebec to leave Confederation;[97] invariably, identification with Quebec is stronger than with Canada.[98] As a group of Quebec franco-phone participants in the 1991 Citizens' Forum on Canada's Future argued: "Quebec is not a region, it is a nation."[99] Herein lies a salient difference between BC and Quebec – between a sense of region on the one hand and a sense of constituting a sociological, and poten-tially politically sovereign, nation on the other.

BC participants in the Citizens' Forum on Canada's Future are quoted as saying: "Canada is a vast land covering diverse geographical and ethnic regions. Some regionalism must therefore be accommodated. However, the same factors suggest a need for a strong central govern-ment."[100] David Elkins has observed: "A wide variety of Canadians in BC can express reasoned disagreement with their federal government, its leader, and his party without calling into question their affection for Canada."[101] And Roger Gibbins and Sonia Arrison note, "The dom-inant form of 'western separatism' is frustrated Canadian nationalism, and not an endorsement of any positive vision of an independent West."[102]

When anger was expressed by BC political leaders or opinion lead-ers towards the federal government, it was usually about whether BC was getting its fair share of federal expenditures; or about BC's representation in the Senate or House of Commons under the Char-lottetown proposals; or about whether BC would receive symbolic recognition as a self-standing region of Canada in the immediate after-math of the 1995 Quebec referendum. There is no British Columbia party actively campaigning for an independent BC.[103] Few British Columbians have shown the deep commitment to the idea of a BC nation that so many francophone nationalists have shown to the idea of a Quebec nation over the past forty years. There are provincial politicians, particularly on the NDP side, who have openly voiced concerns about a potential Balkanization of the country stemming from too much whittling away of the powers of the federal government.[104] And BC public opinion, if views about the social union are anything to go by, seems to be divided between support for the right of provinces to opt out of national programs and the right of Ottawa to enforce national standards by itself.[105]

Still, there is in the BC political tradition a residual willingness on the part of some political and opinion leaders to threaten the worst if BC does not get its way. Some of this goes back to anger over the procrastination of the federal government in meeting its railway commitments to the province in the early years of Confederation. Some of this could surface over BC's financial treatment by Ottawa during the Depression years, for example, a 1934 editorial in the *Vancouver Sun* threatening the establishment of "A Dominion of British Columbia."[106] And some of this reflects BC's geographical location on the western periphery of Canada: "So we sit smugly upon our beauty spots, express our confidence that this is the best of all possible lands and that in it we live the best of all possible ways of life, not awfully caring whether Quebec secedes or not, but understanding their feelings and being quietly interested in its mechanics. We can't help thinking that geography would make a parallel operation at the western end of Canada a very logical, neat and tidy affair."[107]

All this helps explain why British Columbia has not contributed in a fulsome manner to the debate about Canadian unity. There have been no federal prime ministers from BC who have ever held that office for more than a few months; nor have cabinet ministers from this province generally wielded the kind of clout that ministers from Quebec or Ontario have had. BC premiers have engaged in the debate about Canadian unity only on a sporadic basis, such as at federal-provincial conferences when the subject has been on the agenda. In many ways, BC has been something of a rich, outlying region of Canada, largely caught up with its own narcissistic pursuits. In the words of Bruce Hutchison: "Vancouver has always thought of little but Vancouver. Always British Columbia thinks of British Columbia."[108]

Moreover, BC has its own internal regional divides, for example, between the Lower Mainland (that is, the Greater Vancouver area), where more than half the population of the province now lives, and the rest of the province.[109] This has sometimes led those living in the Peace region and in parts of the East Kootenays to speak of joining up with Alberta; it has led to occasional calls for Vancouver Island to go it alone,[110] and, for good measure, to calls for an independent Vancouver city-state.[111]

For certain purposes, BC's inhabitants and politicians feel themselves part of western Canada or the West, yet for others they feel themselves apart from the other western provinces, including Alberta. There is a Canadian dimension, but there is also a strong north-south pull, towards Washington, Oregon, and California – a major focus of BC's external trade. Cascadia – a region meant to unite BC, Washington, and Oregon – may be something of a pipe dream as long as the United States is not threatened with imminent breakup,[112] but it speaks to one part of the BC psyche. And there is the pull of the Pacific Rim, even in the wake of the recent economic meltdown in Asia.

British Columbia is a pluralistic, multifaceted society that does not lend itself to easy generalizations. In the words of the Montreal journalist Paul Wells: "The next time somebody comes East over the Rockies to tell you 'what BC wants' don't believe a word of it. BC wants about 1,000 contradictory things at once. Which is another way of saying it's a vibrant, if somewhat chaotic democracy."[113]

BC's economic elites, often the wielders of new fortunes, are above all concerned with the business of moneymaking, wherever that road may lead them. Deep reflections on their province of residence or its culture are not their wont. The members of BC's cultural elites – academics, journalists, writers, filmmakers – unlike their counterparts in Quebec, rarely share any common purpose. It is more difficult to launch common intellectual initiatives in Canada's West Coast province than in either Ontario or Quebec. BC's political leaders remain divided across the ideological divide of right and left, although the exact meaning of such terms may appear more uncertain at the end of the twentieth century than it seemed at its beginning.[114] BC's population has multiple origins and is divided along religious-secular lines, between Aboriginal and non-Aboriginal, by a diversity of ethnic backgrounds, and by various other shades of identity, such as gender or sexual orientation, which loom large in certain urban or university milieus.

Individualism, and with it conflicting rather than overarching communal values, is the dominant characteristic of BC's inhabitants. As Jean Bethke Elshtain has pointed out with reference to the United States, identity politics or what is sometimes called the politics of difference makes the forging of any sense of shared community more difficult.[115] The same would certainly hold true for BC. For his part,

Charles Taylor talks about the need for "horizons of shared signifi-cance" in modern societies riven by the ethos of "doing your own thing."[116] By this standard, BC society is recognizably less communi-tarian or community-minded than Quebec's.

Does a sense of BC's regional distinctiveness, therefore, not exist at all? In answering this question, I am tempted to draw on the reflec-tions of Ernest Gellner, one of the more astute students of nationalism in our day. Regarding cultures, he writes: "Cultures are both tenacious and volatile. It is neither true that they are virtually immutable ... nor is it the case that they are ever reinvented, ever spurious in their pretence of continuity. *Both* things happen, and if there are any laws concerning which predominates, we do not know them."[117]

As for the origins of a phenomenon such as nationalism, he notes facetiously: "My own view is that some nations possess genuine ancient navels, some have navels invented for them by their nation-alist propaganda, and some are altogether navel-less. My own belief is also that the middle category is by far the largest."[118]

In much the same way, one can see BC regionalism as a product partly of continuity, partly of invention; with a navel invented for it by the propagandists of BC regionalism in our own day, as by their predecessors in an earlier one. Yet not all is contrived: there is a gen-uine sense of regional distinctiveness to British Columbia, flowing from its geographical position, its resource economy, its historical development, and its idiosyncratic political traditions. There is a sense of estrangement from central Canada that can be channelled into a politics of resentment. There is the sense of a hybrid community con-tinuously in the making – more oriented to the present and the future than to the past – that strikes even the casual observer of the BC scene. It is this sense of distinctiveness, fractured though it may be, reinvented though it constantly may be, vituperative though it may sometimes be, that this study, with its focus on BC's reaction to the national unity debate, tries to illuminate.

2
British Columbia Political Leaders and Canadian Unity

A brief summary of events relating to Quebec nationalism will help set the stage for the analysis found in Chapters 2 to 4.

Ever since the Quiet Revolution of the 1960s, the question of Quebec's status within Confederation has dominated Canadian political debate. A nascent separatist movement in the 1960s, with its violent offshoot, the Front de libération du Québec (FLQ), set the stage for the establishment of the Royal Commission on Bilingualism and Biculturalism. This in turn led to the passage of the Official Languages Act and to attempts on the part of the federal government to promote official bilingualism as a solution to the Quebec question.

The coming to power of the Parti Québécois (PQ) in 1976 lent new urgency to the debate. A referendum on sovereignty-association was held in Quebec in 1980, with 60 percent of the electorate voting "no" and 40 percent "yes." In the aftermath of the "no" victory, both Prime Minister Pierre Trudeau and the federalist side were committed to undertaking a major reform of the Canadian constitution.

These constitutional negotiations went through several phases, culminating in November 1981 in an agreement between the federal government and nine of the provinces to a package combining patriation, the Canadian Charter of Rights and Freedoms, and a new amending formula. Quebec under René Lévesque found itself isolated.

The Quebec question did not go away for all that. On the contrary, the election of a Conservative government under Brian Mulroney in 1984, followed in short order by the return of a Liberal government in Quebec headed by Robert Bourassa, led to a new round of constitutional debate. This culminated in the Meech Lake Accord of 1987, which recognized Quebec as a distinct society within Canada and gave somewhat greater powers to all the provinces.

After the Bourassa government's invocation of the "notwithstanding clause" in December 1988, overturning the Supreme Court of Canada's ruling permitting the use of both English and French on commercial signs in Quebec, public opinion in Canada outside Quebec turned strongly against the accord. The upshot, despite a marathon round of negotiations in Ottawa in June 1990, was the demise of Meech Lake.

The two years that followed witnessed further constitutional deliberations, resulting in the Charlottetown Accord of August 1992. In a national referendum on 26 October 1992, 54.5 percent of Canadians voted against the agreement. The strongest opposition came from British Columbia, where 68 percent voted "no."

The election of a PQ government in September 1994 led to the holding of a second Quebec referendum, this time on sovereignty-partnership, in October 1995. This turned out to be a much closer call than in 1980, with 49.4 percent supporting the "yes" side and 50.6 percent the "no." The referendum thus served as something of a wake-up call for the rest of Canada as far as the prospect of Quebec separation was concerned.

In November 1995, the federal government introduced a resolution in Parliament recognizing Quebec as a distinct society. In hewing to a four-region model of Canada – the Atlantic provinces, Quebec, Ontario, and the West – where veto powers were concerned, however, the Chrétien government provoked a firestorm in BC. This resulted in a revamped resolution that recognized BC as one of the five regions of Canada in its own right.

The federal government subsequently referred the constitutional legalities of Quebec secession to the Supreme Court of Canada, which came down with its carefully weighed decision in August 1998. And the premiers of the nine provinces outside Quebec agreed to the Calgary Declaration in September 1997, which combined recognition of Quebec's unique character with the principle of the equality of all the provinces.

And here matters rest in the aftermath of the re-election of a PQ government in Quebec in November 1998, albeit with a smaller share of the popular vote than in 1994. What all this augurs in terms of a possible future Quebec referendum, particularly if the "yes" side wins, is something to which I will turn in the final chapter of this book.

What I would like to do in this chapter is present a snapshot of the position taken by BC premiers and leading BC politicians with respect to the following:

- Quebec demands from the 1960s to the Calgary Declaration of 1997
- the role of the federal government and federal institutions
- BC's distinctiveness as a region
- BC separatism
- the BC vision of Canada.

To this end, I shall make use of statements made by BC premiers to federal-provincial conferences and similar forums, and of other speeches and statements by leading BC politicians from the 1960s through the 1990s. The purpose of this exercise, simply put, is to assess the official BC contribution to the Canadian unity debate.

Quebec

BC politicians have waxed hot and cold on the question of Quebec's position within Confederation. As early as 1963, W.A.C. Bennett became the first provincial premier to speak out against any concessions to Quebec nationalism:

> If any people have wrongs they should be righted. But as far as any changes in the British North America Act or the 1871 agreement under which we entered Confederation, we will not listen or agree to any basic changes in Confederation at any time.[1]

He also opposed equalization payments to provinces like Quebec:

> The Government of Canada has paid out over $5,500,000,000 in equalization payments since their introduction in 1957, and they continue to increase substantially each year. One province, Quebec, received 47 per cent of this amount. There is little evidence these unconditional grants, which have been paid to certain provincial governments, have increased the relative standard of living of the citizens in the areas in which they have been received.[2]

In the run-up to the two Quebec referenda in 1980 and 1995, BC politicians made clear their refusal of any type of sovereignty-association or sovereignty-partnership arrangement with that province:

> I would be remiss if I did not restate my firm opposition to the concept of "sovereignty-association." [It] offers British Columbians no spirit, no heart, no common purpose, and no goals. The bottom line of nationhood

is not to be found on a balance sheet ... Remove nationhood and the commitment to sacrifice some regional advantages goes with it ... A sovereign Quebec would become a foreign country with whom we would treat exclusively on a basis of self-interest.[3]

If somebody tried to break up this country, we would be the worst of enemies. It's not going to be civilized. It's not going to be over tea with our pinkies out.[4]

There can be no illusion about the depth of resentment Quebec's departure from Canada would be likely to provoke from any future BC government.

Nor have BC politicians shown much sympathy for the notion of special status for Quebec:

I am not proposing "special status" for Quebec.[5]

All Canadians must be equal.[6]

Distinct society for Quebec. I don't have a clue what it means and won't agree to its entrenchment.[7]

I don't think there should be any special status for Quebec. BC, as the fastest growing province, has to be very careful about enshrining any special rights for a province.[8]

There is something of a zero-sum game involved where any acknowledgment of Quebec's special character by BC politicians is concerned and the view they hold of British Columbia's place in the larger Canadian equation.

BC politicians have generally been fulsome in their support for national unity, however:

The Government of the Province of British Columbia is firmly committed to the concept of a united Canada and to the principles of the Canadian Confederation.[9]

I assure you, the people of British Columbia want the great province of Quebec to stay within Canada, to continue to enrich our country by all it has to offer and be enriched in return by the rest of Canada.[10]

The very unity of our country is greatly threatened. I don't want to see Canada break up – and you don't either.[11]

British Columbians, Honourable Speaker, are passionate Canadians, and stalwart supporters of national unity.[12]

Faced with the prospect of the country's demise, BC politicians have allowed the Canadian chord to resonate more loudly and clearly than when more narrowly BC concerns have been at stake.

There has been some openness on the part of BC politicians to accommodating the linguistic and cultural concerns of Quebec, provided this stops short of special status:

The province of Quebec is and always will be the homeland in Canada of the French language and culture ... Quebec should have some flexibility on matters of language and culture ... To give one part of Canada the power to enhance the language and culture of its choice is not inconsistent with the concept of Canadian nationhood.[13]

I have a bit more sympathy [towards Quebec] if you could define the question of language and culture.[14]

There have also been statements hostile to Quebec, however. Most striking was the one in 1977 by Bill Vander Zalm, then minister of human resources in the Social Credit government:

Certainly I wouldn't lose any sleep if Quebec separates. I doubt, frankly, if there are too many people who will lose very much sleep if they were to separate. I don't think it matters much ... The decision to separate, I don't think it is all that bad. For one thing, I'm sure there will be considerable savings to the populace generally, that we won't have to have two printings on every cornflakes box, or whatever it might be.[15]

And there has been considerable frustration over the degree to which Quebec dominates the federal agenda:

It's time to abandon the game that's been played in this country for some time. Everybody is supposed to be quiet and support the federal government because of this Quebec presence, and not deal with any other concerns of this country.[16]

BC issues are viewed by the Central Canadian media through the prism of Quebec's concerns.[17]

In other words, there is a good deal of resentment over the way in which the threat of Quebec separation has crowded out more concerns more specific to British Columbia or to Canada outside Quebec.

Another characteristic of BC politicians has been a tendency to suggest parallels between Quebec and BC when it comes to asserting regional interests:

I think it would be wrong to read into what happened in British Columbia [in the 1975 election] and what has happened in Quebec [in the 1976 election] that these provinces wish to leave the country ... the realities of Canada today are going to demand a new type of federalism, a regional federalism, that more properly will allow the provinces and the regions of this country to develop their own destinies – not separate from Canada but in concert with each other.[18]

British Columbia and Quebec have much in common.[19]

Quebec wants many of the same things as British Columbia, namely greater freedom to manage its economy and no more federal encroachment in the provincial sphere.[20]

The people of British Columbia and the people of Quebec share a similar desire for change.[21]

British Columbia is a province that has long aspired, like Quebec, to have a greater measure of autonomy and self-determination over areas that are of peculiar interest to our future and our destiny.[22]

Now there is something to the parallel where questions of provincial powers are concerned. I believe, however, that a certain amount of self-delusion on the part of BC politicians is also involved. For the BC position and that of recent provincial governments in Quebec are not one and the same. BC politicians, whatever their stripe, see their province as a region, not as a would-be nation, within Canada: "We can be an example to Quebec that fighting for what you want within the country can result in positive steps."[23] By comparison, Quebec governments, both Liberal and PQ, demand a degree of recognition from Ottawa and the other provinces that goes considerably beyond anything BC has ever asked for.

Something of the quite different BC outlook is reflected in the positions adopted by successive BC governments towards the federal government.

The Federal Government and Federal Institutions

The speeches made by BC premiers and intergovernmental affairs ministers at federal-provincial conferences and similar forums over the past three decades recall the litany of complaints voiced by earlier BC premiers such as Richard McBride or Duff Pattullo.

In 1971, W.A.C. Bennett demanded an annual grant of $500 million from the government of Canada to compensate British Columbia for what it was losing through annual federal equalization grants, national tariff policy, federal railway subsidies, and federal hydroelectric development subsidies.[24] In 1973, Dave Barrett highlighted the province's geographical remoteness from the national capital and federal decision making, which he claimed resulted in a lack of appreciation at the federal level of BC's needs and aspirations.[25] In 1976, Bill Bennett demanded that the federal government transfer some of its taxing capacity for mature shared-cost programs to the provinces.[26] In 1986, Bill Vander Zalm reeled off federal procurement, federal enterprise expenditures, and federal government employment per capita as areas where BC was not getting its "fair share" compared with other provinces.[27] He also had plans to introduce a "Confederation Equity Act" to measure federal expenditures in BC against the national average on a scale from 0 to 100, although this legislation never saw the light of day.[28] A decade later, intergovernmental affairs minister Andrew Petter complained about discriminatory practices by the federal government towards BC, citing the cap on Canada Assistance Plan transfers to the province and the penalty imposed on BC for introducing a three-month residence requirement for welfare recipients.[29]

Some of this reflects the concerns of a rich province feeling that it is being asked to carry a disproportionate share of the cost of transfer payments to poorer ones. Some of this reflects a sense of geographical alienation – the price of British Columbia's distance from the federal seat of power.

A persistent refrain has been a call for recognition of BC as a distinct region of Canada. In 1969, W.A.C. Bennett revived a demand that Duff Pattullo had first articulated in the 1930s, that BC be recognized as a self-standing region.[30] In 1978, his son Bill returned to the attack, unveiling a detailed proposal for reform of the Senate, the Supreme Court of Canada, and federal boards and commissions based upon a five-region Canada.[31] And all three BC political leaders rose up in angry protest in the aftermath of the federal government's resolution of November 1995 recognizing Quebec as a distinct society and providing for constitutional vetoes based on a four-region Canada – Atlantic Canada, Quebec, Ontario, and the West. The federal government backed off, recognizing BC as a fifth region where future constitutional changes would be concerned.[32] For BC politicians such as Andrew Petter, however, this grudging recognition amounted to little more than tokenism:

> British Columbians reacted swiftly and angrily when the original four-region veto proposal failed to recognize our province as a region in its own right ... The federal response, moving to five regions, did not alter the fact that any regional veto scheme is inherently flawed ... The federal government should get back on course with positive and practical policy choices ... addressing real issues of concern to Canadians.[33]

I would argue that the desire for recognition as a self-standing region of Canada articulated by a number of different BC governments stems from a pent-up resentment over the relatively backseat role British Columbia has been playing in Confederation ever since 1871.

Underlying the suspicion of federal institutions on the part of BC politicians is an old hinterland-metropolis complex. W.A.C. Bennett spoke of BC as "a goblet to be drained."[34] For Bill Bennett, "the people out here feel a hundred years of resentment that they were a colony within a country."[35] Gordon Campbell saw "BC as the West, Alberta, Saskatchewan and Manitoba as the Near East, Ontario and Quebec as the Mideast, and everything past that as the Far East."[36] Glen Clark bemoaned the fact that "for the national media, a Western Canadian statesman is someone who comes from Western Canada and takes the Ontario or central Canadian perspective."[37] And Senator Pat Carney denounced the tendency of the Eastern press to view British Columbians as fat cats whose list of concerns constitute just another laundry list.[38]

Yet there have been times when BC politicians were quite supportive of the use of federal powers or of specific federal governments or initiatives. Dave Barrett, true to his socialist principles, argued for bringing Canada's energy resources under public ownership and federal control in the mid-1970s.[39] Bill Bennett welcomed the Mulroney government as the first national government in years that represented all regions of the country.[40] Bill Vander Zalm was an enthusiastic supporter of the Canada–United States Free Trade Agreement, decrying its opponents "as badly misreading the mood and will of Canadians, particularly those in Western Canada."[41] Mike Harcourt was an equally enthusiastic supporter of the ill-fated Charlottetown Accord of 1992, which he saw as "promoting political stability for this nation at a time when other countries around the world are tearing themselves apart."[42] And Glen Clark signed on to the social union in February 1999, stating: "I'm taking a different approach than on some issues and trying to be constructive. Substantially, I'll be supporting the federal government. I'm not going there with a big shopping list of demands."[43]

So the attitude of BC political leaders towards the federal government and federal initiatives bespeaks something of a love-hate relationship rather than pure, unbridled antagonism. It is rooted in considerable resentment of BC's second-class status within Confederation, especially when compared with the status of Ontario or Quebec. Indeed, nothing can get the adrenaline flowing more quickly than any perceived slight to BC's aspiration to be seen as a self-standing and important region of Canada. In practice, however, BC premiers are prepared to sign on to most federal initiatives and to refrain from pressing their anti-federal posturing beyond a certain point. When they overstep those limits, as Glen Clark was perceived to do during his three years in office, they may even pay a high political price for it. Quebec premiers, by comparison, pay a high price when they are seen to be inadequate defenders of Quebec's interests.

British Columbia as a Distinct Region

Regional distinctiveness has played an evolving role in BC political discourse.

W.A.C. Bennett was one of the first to signal a Pacific Rim vocation for the province. British Columbia, he argued in the early 1960s, was not interested in restricting its export trade to old alliances. Rather, it sought to pursue new trade frontiers throughout the Americas and in the Pacific region.[44] In other speeches, he noted the province's phenomenal population growth, twice the percentage for the rest of Canada. One aspect of this was the large number of social assistance recipients and retired people moving to BC from other provinces, which placed greater demands on the BC government for social services. No other region in Canada was confronted by such a problem.[45]

Under Dave Barrett, the BC government tended to highlight its commitment to social security and health care. It urged the federal government to recognize the legislative priority of the provinces in the field of social security and to give them sufficient resources to carry this out.[46] While emphasizing the unique problems that BC faced and that required redress, however, the Barrett government was significantly less inclined to wrap itself in the mantle of aggrieved region than its Social Credit counterparts.[47] In fact, it argued the importance of national programs with national standards in areas such as health care, and the need to avoid any Balkanization of the country.[48] It was even prepared to surrender oil and natural gas rights granted to the province under the constitution if the federal government assumed control over the country's petroleum industry.[49] Between 1972 and 1975, BC's distinctiveness took second place to a more national perspective.

With the return to power of Social Credit in December 1975, the provincial government sounded a very different note. "My province is distinct in its history, in its peoples, in its economic thrust, and partly distinct in its cultures, from other regions of Canada. It is even distinct from the rest of Western Canada," Bill Bennett declared.[50] Some of this claim to distinctiveness was related to the economic policies his government would follow: an emphasis on restraining government expenditure and public sector compensation,[51] a call for governmental deregulation,[52] and a high priority placed on remaining competitive both domestically and in export markets.[53] It led to the restraint measures of 1983-84, which Bennett himself characterized as "a difficult and painful process of adjustment" for his province.[54] At the same time, the premier underlined the importance of the Pacific Rim for BC growth and trade.[55] He demanded greater provincial input into the making of national economic policies.[56] And he unveiled his own five-region proposal for constitutional change, which was alluded to earlier.

Bill Vander Zalm spelled out his view of BC's distinctiveness at his very first federal-provincial conference in 1986:

> You know the geography of Canada is a strange thing from the point of view of British Columbia ... It's almost as if we're looking at each other through different ends of the same telescope – we see Ottawa without difficulty whereas from the East, BC at times seems somehow diminished in scale and size, and as a result, in importance.[57]

Vander Zalm opposed the constitutional entrenchment of Aboriginal self-government, seeing it as a source of division within the province most affected by Aboriginal demands.[58] He set as one of his government's goals "establishing British Columbia as North America's gateway to the Pacific Rim,"[59] and argued the need for the province "to look westward and welcome the opportunities offered by the fundamental economic shift toward the Pacific Rim."[60] In matters constitutional, he ultimately supported the Meech Lake Accord, in no small part because he saw it as weakening the powers of the federal government.[61] He sought to amend the accord, however, to recognize the unique characteristics of each of the provinces, not just of Quebec.[62] He touched another populist chord by introducing provisions for referenda on constitutional questions into the BC legislature.[63] And along with the Reform Party he argued the case for a "triple-E" Senate as BC's number one constitutional priority.[64]

The return of the NDP to power in October 1991 did not mark the eclipse of regionalism in BC political discourse. Instead, regionalism played a not unimportant role in Mike Harcourt's defence of the Charlottetown Accord. He spoke about a Canada

> where the regions are dealt in with revitalized democratic institutions ... [where] Canadians in every region of our nation can have greater power to manage and develop their provincial economies and empower communities to build local economies ... [where] British Columbians – and people in all our nation's regions – can have significant new political clout in the revitalized and renewed two-House Parliament.[65]

He returned to the charge on the evening of the 1995 Quebec referendum, arguing that "we all want a country that recognizes our regional differences, and that frees us from the straight jacket of an overly centralized government in Ottawa."[66]

His successor was even more given to playing defender of BC's specificity:

> I'm not part of this constitutional industry, but the notion of two founding nations is something that is completely foreign to my background. We have 400,000 Chinese-Canadians in BC. So, if it ever was two founding nations – I don't believe it was – but if it ever was, it certainly isn't now.[67]

In Clark's opinion, "proposals put forward to foster unity could not be narrowly focused on Quebec."[68] For his minister of intergovernmental affairs, Andrew Petter, the Quebec referendum

> gave birth not just to a new regionalism but to a real serious questioning of the federal agenda, a sense that we went through 10 years of hell trying to accommodate Quebec. That we were now going to be more assertive about our own interests.[69]

According to Petter, fiscal favouritism towards needy provinces was corroding the attachment of BC towards federal policies: "There has to be a sense there is equity among regions, a sense that there is equity among individuals."[70] Or, as he put it when he introduced the Calgary Declaration into the BC legislature, "British Columbians have a keen sense of our own identity, and of the things that distinguish us from the rest of the country."[71]

The regional refrain, in other words, runs deep and across party lines. Its most frequently cited components include British Columbia's Pacific vocation, its unique economic base, its cultural distinctiveness even when compared with the other western provinces, and the increasingly multicultural character of its population. Where provincial politicians are concerned, regionalism can clearly serve as a justification for claiming greater powers for the province vis-à-vis Ottawa. And it can serve another very important purpose – as a foil to Quebec's demands for recognition of its own distinct character. For if Quebec is to be regarded as distinct, so the argument goes, why not British Columbia as well?

BC Separatism

Just how far might the sense of a distinct BC identity go? There has always been a current of separatism in British Columbia, going back to the period following BC's entry into Confederation and complaints over delays in the completion of the transcontinental railway, and surfacing again during the Great Depression of the 1930s. In the contemporary period, when the issue of Quebec separation has been very much on the agenda, the idea of BC going on its own has been raised again as an option for the future.

Where BC politicians have been concerned, this separatist current could take latent or explicit forms. W.A.C. Bennett was known to say that British Columbia was the only part of Canada that would be able to survive alone or would dare to try it.[72] Then there was Pat McGeer, minister of education in the Social Credit governments between 1975 and 1986. In 1977 he told the legislature that the federal government should have only those powers given to it by the unanimous consent of the provinces – a BC version of the 1991 Allaire Report of the Quebec Liberal Party, which would have reduced the federal government to something of a shell. Gordon Gibson, the BC Liberal leader at the time, criticized McGeer for a proposal that would amount to the effective dismemberment of Canada.[73] In 1980 McGeer was cited as one of several Social Credit ministers, along with Rafe Mair, who unblushingly endorsed the idea of a separate BC: "In Quebec the people almost had to vote against the referendum in order not to become poor. Here, if we had one, the people would almost have to vote in favor of it in order to become rich."[74]

Similar musings surfaced in the aftermath of the Meech Lake and Charlottetown Accords and the 1995 Quebec referendum. "British Columbians must consider separating from Canada," former BC Liberal leader Gordon Wilson declared in April 1994. He said that Canadians would respect West Coast interests only if they knew that British Columbians, like Quebecers, were ready to go it alone:

> They have to know that people in British Columbia are serious ... If we don't deem that our interests will continue to be served in Canada, then we would have to ... set up some kind of independent status for the province. The situation would get worse in an Ontario-dominated Canada if Quebec departs.[75]

An independent British Columbia was one of the options considered in a 1997 study commissioned by Gordon Wilson, by then the leader of the Progressive Democratic Alliance and advisor to Premier Clark on constitutional matters. In the words of the author of this study, Gordon Gibson, himself a former BC Liberal leader (and one-time critic of Pat McGeer!):

> The option [of an independent British Columbia] would work perfectly well, in both economic and political terms. There is no doubt on the economic side – our situation would be very healthy ... There is no doubt but what [sic] leaders exist in British Columbia with the necessary talent to lead an independent country.[76]

In September 1997, Senator and former federal cabinet minister Pat Carney entered the fray. Upset by the salmon wars between BC and

Ottawa, and convinced that a central Canadian ethic was being imposed upon the province, she argued that BC needed to renegotiate its relationship with Canada and not rule out separation: "Playing by the rules is not going to get their attention."[77] For weeks thereafter, the media, both provincial and national, were filled with heated reactions to her statement evoking separation.

By and large, BC premiers and ministers of intergovernmental affairs have not advocated secession. For all his Ottawa-bashing over the Columbia River Treaty or his proposals for a BC-based bank, W.A.C. Bennett was wont to proclaim that "the premier is a Canadian, first, last, and all the time. We will never break the British connection as long as I am premier."[78] Bill Bennett, while certainly a staunch "BC-firster" in his own right, made clear on more than one occasion that "his party stands committed to Canada";[79] "there is no way I could be part of those who would cut and run."[80] Bill Vander Zalm, in an interview shortly after becoming premier, described himself as "very Canadian."[81] In 1990 he declared: "It's not separation. We're not talking separation. We're talking about greater decentralization."[82] (It is worth noting, however, that Vander Zalm may have been friendlier to the idea of an independent BC off the record than on it. "It would not take much to awaken the separatist spirit in Bill Vander Zalm," wrote the authors of a 1989 book on Vander Zalm, citing members of Vander Zalm's immediate entourage.[83]) Glen Clark, no patsy when it came to his relations with Ottawa, could also state that "the country is in a very fragile state. The country is deeply challenged financially and in terms of regional tensions. It's important that we don't stand up for BC in a way that is destructive to the nation."[84] Andrew Petter, reacting to the 1997 report tabled by Gordon Wilson, commented: "Talk of joining with Alberta, going it alone, or hitching BC's wagon to some American states can be counter-productive. It sends the wrong signal to Quebec."[85] The fact remains, however, that BC separatism, while a good deal weaker than its counterpart in Quebec, is a sentiment that politicians, both in Victoria and Ottawa, must reckon with from time to time, and that at least some BC politicians have actively helped to fan. It has resurfaced, at least rhetorically, in the context of the current debate about Canadian unity.

A British Columbia Vision of Canada?

Is there then a BC vision of Canada? How do BC politicians, given their strongly provincialist leanings and a strong sense of regionalism in the province, view the country as whole? There is no simple answer to these questions, but this section examines the positions articulated by BC political leaders in recent decades.

One of the more striking features of BC politicians is their ability to play regional champion and Canadian patriot at one and the same time. David Mitchell, a biographer of W.A.C. Bennett and a former member of the BC legislature, notes:

> Was Bennett a kind of proto-separatist? Or was he just giving expression to the peculiar form of isolationism which was part of the Pacific coast heritage? It seems clear that he was simply exploiting a traditional Western Canadian streak of independence and resentment towards Central Canada, enhanced now by BC's new economic viability. Certainly, Bennett challenged many established assumptions about Confederation, but he was always talking about improving the country, making Canada a better place to live, and he often painted himself as a kind of supernationalist.[86]

His son Bill insisted on the need to restructure the national government "in order to bring Canada's regions into the process of national decision-making," arguing that the federation would emerge from the process "strengthened, more enriched and more unified."[87] Or, as he put it in a speech in Montreal a week before the May 1980 Quebec referendum, "We in British Columbia don't want to 'opt out' of Canada. On the contrary, our goal is to 'opt in,' in a new and more meaningful way than has ever been the case before."[88] Bill Vander Zalm vigorously argued the case for British Columbia's "fair share" of federal expenditures, castigating what he perceived as "favouritism towards Central Canada."[89] This in no way undermined his "unwavering recognition that Canada should remain a strong, free, and united country."[90] Gordon Wilson could threaten to "fight for my province to stand alone in the world" if the Canadian ideal floundered, yet in the same breath speak of his "commitment to the fight to keep Canada together."[91] Andrew Petter vigorously argued that "from BC's point of view, the discrimination that exists in areas [of social transfers] are really national unity issues, the clearest signals that the federal government doesn't view British Columbia on the basis of equality, as a full player in Canada."[92] He could also suggest, however, that British Columbians' commitment both to greater provincial autonomy and to effective central government made them "uniquely positioned to act as a bridge between competing interests and visions that have sometimes divided this country in the past."[93]

There is nothing untoward about combining regional and national loyalties in one's vision of country. In a federal system, this is something to be expected. But one can legitimately ask whether BC politicians project a specifically Canadian vision as opposed to simply trying to enhance their own particular, regional interests. Central to W.A.C. Bennett's vision of Canada was a country divided into five economic zones, with British Columbia's territory extending northward to include the Yukon. To those who might criticize his motives, he would petulantly respond:

> I am going to tell you at one time Ontario was a very small Province. You got all your northern territories. Why not British Columbia? Why not the Prairies, my friend? Fair treatment to one; fair treatment to all.[94]

No wonder Tommy Douglas, a fellow premier at the time, was moved to observe about Bennett:

> He would know what BC's problems were better than anybody around the table. But one never felt that he understood the larger picture – what it is that makes Canada tick, what it is that keeps Confederation together, and what is likely to destroy it.[95]

The same may also be true of other BC political leaders, with the signal exceptions of Dave Barrett and Mike Harcourt. Bill Bennett, premier from 1975 to 1986, opposed status quo federalism in the name of a new type of regional federalism, arguing the case for a five-region Canada at the 1978 First Ministers' Conference.[96] In 1980 he noted that "Canada is more than the sum of the ten provinces and territories, but Canadians do not live in a place called 'federal,' they live in PEI, in Quebec, in Saskatchewan, in British Columbia. That is why the voices of the provinces must be heard loud and clear in this process of amending our constitution."[97] And his minister of intergovernmental affairs, Garde Gardom, in opposing the unilateral actions of the Trudeau government in the constitutional field, summoned up "an all-powerful, almost totally centralistically governed state" as the model that the federal government seemed to be springing on the provinces.[98] If Bill Bennett had a message for the rest of Canada, however, it lay less in any political remaking of the federation and more in the tough fiscal policies he would pursue after 1983. As one of his backbenchers put it:

Other free enterprise governments in future years – not only across Canada but through the United States and around the world – will follow the example of this Premier and his government in BC in dealing with the civil service the way they did in this budget.[99]

Bill Vander Zalm favoured a radical restructuring of Confederation in a decentralizing direction:

We're talking about greater decentralization, we're talking about a redistribution, we're talking about a greater degree of accountability closer to the people. I don't think we could ever fare to the maximum of our ability as long as the rules continue to be made in Quebec and Ontario because of the tremendous impact of the structure of government and the makeup of the bureaucracy.[100]

Under the circumstances, there was little room in his thinking for the more federal side of the Canadian equation.

When a BC premier like Mike Harcourt tried to place national interest above purely regional interest, as was undoubtedly true in the case of the Charlottetown Accord, his stand could quickly run afoul of public opinion in his province.[101] "Premier Bonehead" was the term his critics invented to describe his weak bargaining stance where BC interests were concerned – a term that stuck with him throughout his remaining years in office. A chastened Harcourt noted in his memoirs:

Instead of becoming actively engaged [in the Charlottetown negotiations], I should have offered advice and counsel when it was requested. Perhaps, I should have restricted my involvement to providing a clear baseline, or final position on the issues. In effect, let the rest of them come to us. Perhaps I should have ignored the brilliance of the constitutional spotlight ... But I had picked up a skill for conflict resolution over the years. To use it now, if you will, to help save Canada, seemed a perfectly reasonable thing to do at the time.[102]

No wonder his successor was much more circumspect about touching the constitutional dossier. As he told the BC Unity Panel set up in the aftermath of the Calgary Declaration:

This is not about the constitution. If it's about the constitution then we'll get into a debate about the language and a constitutional deal with

Quebec would not pass referendum in BC at this time. Therefore, discussion about constitutional amendment is not useful at this time.[103]

As for the leader of the opposition, Gordon Campbell, his approach to federal-provincial relations is fairly narrow. In the words of a journalist who has interviewed him on the subject, "The Liberal leader's philosophy is fiercely fiscal. For Campbell, federal-provincial relations is less about nation building than budget balancing."[104]

So where does this leave us? At the very minimum with a sense of the clear limitations of the vision that BC politicians project beyond their own province. There is a larger Canada out there, but it only periodically stirs the imaginations of those mandated to speak in the province's name. An emphasis on BC's distinctiveness invariably accompanies any acknowledgment of the larger Canadian universe. A sense of grievance about BC's place in the councils of power in Ottawa or about an unfair allocation of federal expenditures overshadows political debate. Under the circumstances, there is only limited sympathy for Quebec's demands and a prickly reaction to any suggestion of special status for that province. Not for nothing have Canadian prime ministers been known to complain that British Columbians dwell at the foot of a mountain but never trek to the top,[105] or that BC is almost as difficult to handle as Quebec.[106] It says something about the mind-set of so many of its political leaders that this should be so.

Conclusion

There has been a strongly regionalist tone to the sentiments of BC politicians over the past forty years, especially where Social Credit governments – that is, politicians on the right of the political spectrum – have been concerned. In contrast, NDP politicians like Dave Barrett and, to a lesser degree, Mike Harcourt, have tended to play the regionalist motif less aggressively, although the NDP government of Glen Clark was characterized by an Ottawa-bashing tone – on the question of the salmon fishery, on that of social assistance to non-BC residents – that would have done a W.A.C. Bennett proud. Where regionalist posturing is concerned, the right-left cleavage may be less important today than in an earlier period, when it was a major element in the polarization of provincial politics.

BC is very much a "have" province, and in the end this may have more influence on the position adopted by BC governments than the stripe of the party in power in Victoria. It is a province whose political elite is conscious of its geographical location on the western periphery of Canada, of its shifting demography, and of the new openings that the Asia-Pacific arena represents for the future. It is a province whose politicians have never invested large political or intellectual resources into the task of nation building at the Canadian level.

By and large, BC politicians eschew separatism for their own province, just as they do for Quebec, but they have not contributed very much to the national unity debate. The case can be made that Alberta, under premiers like Peter Lougheed or Ralph Klein, or at the federal level through figures like Joe Clark and Preston Manning, has played a more meaningful role in staking out a western Canadian position than politicians from western Canada's most populous province.[107] It is as though a sense of regional distinctiveness, or perhaps location on the far western limits of Canada, has prevented a more proactive role by BC politicians in national debates; at best, BC politicians *react* to Quebec challenges and federal initiatives.

Is this likely to change any time soon? Not in the goldfish-bowl atmosphere of BC politics, where any sign of weakness in defending regional interests can lead to sharp denunciation, not only by opposition parties but also by journalists with piranha instincts. Not in the adversarial game that has defined the BC-Canadian relationship for so long, with provincial governments of different persuasions keen to wrest greater powers from the central government. It may yet turn out, however, that in this respect BC politicians are out of synch with important currents of opinion in the province. The next two chapters explore how BC opinion-makers and BC public opinion at large react to the same five themes that have been examined in this chapter. It will quickly become apparent that while some British Columbians may share with their provincial politicians a vitriolic resentment towards Ottawa, others in BC are no less resentful of these very politicians, whom they see as fuelling regional discontent.

3
British Columbia Opinion-Makers and Canadian Unity

Whatever their strengths or limitations, BC politicians are one part of a story that needs to be told. It is also important, however, to take into account the views of a wider range of BC opinion-makers on the subjects of Canadian unity and BC's place within the Canadian federation.

In some of the recent social science literature, the figures on whom I want to focus in this chapter might be equated with the term "civil society." I have problems with the overuse of this term, which has become something of a catchall in contemporary debates for all manner of non-governmental activity.[1] Instead, I prefer to speak of opinion-makers, *by which I mean those who can be said to influence or shape public opinion in Canada's Pacific province.* The views of ordinary British Columbians, in contradistinction to such opinion-makers, are looked at more closely in the next chapter.

When I speak of BC opinion-makers, then, whom exactly do I have in mind? In part, the representatives of organized interest groups such as business, labour, environmental organizations, or multicultural communities; in part, journalists, commentators, and editorial writers for major newspapers and magazines; in part, advisors to government, experts, and academics; in part, authors/writers, professionals, and others who have made their views on BC and Canada publicly known.

One thing that struck me as I surveyed the material on which this chapter draws is the extreme diversity of views that is reflected. There are passionate defenders of a strong role for the federal government; of an open, accommodating attitude towards Quebec; of a British Columbia that pulls its weight in the national unity debate. There are equally strong proponents of the devolution of power to the provinces; of a tough-minded attitude towards a Quebec that has been hogging the national limelight for all too long; of a BC-first rather than Canada-first approach to the question of collective identity. Nor do these two clusters capture the entire spectrum of opinion. There are many shades of grey among the opinion-makers, reflecting both Canadian and British Columbian predilections in the positions that they take. And opinion-makers can wax hot or cold as the situation dictates, deadly serious or purposely lighthearted, driven by a sense of historical grievance or buoyed up by the unlimited possibilities that the future seems to offer. There is no one view of British Columbia's place in the larger Canadian scheme of things, no one view on how to react to the national unity crisis. This, in and of itself, may be symptomatic of the more equivocal role that regionalism plays for British Columbia opinion-makers than nationalism plays in the *Weltanschauung* of Quebec opinion-makers.

In analyzing the views of BC opinion-makers, I propose to use the same rubric that I adopted in examining the attitudes of BC political leaders in Chapter 2. Rather than looking at individuals or groups in their own right, I will try to make sense of a range of opinions that has been expressed over the past couple of decades in terms of five basic categories:

- views on Quebec
- the role of the federal government and federal institutions
- BC's distinctiveness as a region
- BC separatism
- the BC vision of Canada.

Some have written extensively on these topics, others only episodically; some views merit closer attention, others only passing reference. While I can hardly claim to be exhaustive, I have tried hard in the sampling that follows to ensure that those I quote are drawn from as wide a range of opinion-makers as possible.

Quebec

The persistent challenges that Quebec has posed to Canadian unity have sparked strongly negative responses from a number of BC opinion-makers. For Rafe Mair, former Social Credit cabinet minister and currently a radio talk show host,

Quebec has convinced itself that it's being shortchanged in its association with Canada, though the precise opposite is easily demonstrated ... If we retain Quebec's presence through appeasement, special treatment and continuing bribes, we will not gain her affection, respect or loyalty. We will simply whet her appetite for separation.[2]

To those who say that a special designation for Quebec doesn't necessarily mean a Quebec veto I reply, "If you believe that, you'll believe anything."[3]

For Mel Smith, constitutional advisor to successive BC Social Credit governments,

The concept of the equality of provinces is strongly held among provinces and their peoples, and the prospects for a radically asymmetrical model ... to meet Quebec's demands are not likely achievable or desirable ... One needs to seriously question the validity of any claim for still more special status for Quebec which is based on the argument that the French language and culture lack protection.[4]

For Cyril Shelford, a cabinet minister in the W.A.C. Bennett years, "it's time we forgot about special rights and all become just Canadians – and proud of it."[5] Pat McGeer, a cabinet minister in the Bill Bennett governments, declared, "As a passionate Canadian, I will be voting against the Charlottetown Accord because it is all about special privileges and ignores equal treatment."[6]

For *British Columbia Report,* a magazine close to the Reform Party and a vociferous opponent of both the Meech Lake and Charlottetown Accords:

Quebec should decide what it wants to do once and for all. If it opts to leave, then by all means leave ... though Quebec ought not to assume that we will acquiesce if large areas of the province, in particular the north, elect to remain in Canada ... But the one outcome we do not want is that of perpetual uncertainty ... The other provinces should initiate a constitutional amendment spelling out the terms which any province should meet if it seeks to secede.[7]

For the *Vancouver Sun,* Quebec separatism was nothing short of racist:

Mr. Bouchard and his fellow separatists have got it exactly upside down. Canada is a country – a modern country whose ties transcend ethnicity and language. It's the republican Quebec of Mr. Bouchard's feverish dream that's unreal – racially based, xenophobic and chest-thumping. The models, for those, like Mr. Bouchard, eager to march backward toward tribalism are the bloodied, broken non-countries of the world like Lebanon, Northern Ireland and the former Yugoslavia.[8]

And in an editorial following the re-election of the Parti Québécois government in November 1998, the paper argued: "Neither Ottawa nor the other provinces should concede special leverage to Quebec. It is just another province, like BC, trying to get more out of Ottawa."[9]

Resentment runs like a red thread through these statements. Quebec is pushing for special privileges that no other province aspires to; it is ethnocentric; it is racist; it is an accomplished practitioner of blackmail. Under no circumstances should British Columbians or their government be conned into granting Quebec the kind of exclusive recognition its nationalist leaders demand.

Others have taken a more muted approach. Mary Collins, a former Conservative federal cabinet minister, observed that "Westerners are not prepared to make any kind of conciliatory gesture. My concern is that Quebec is getting more and more isolated."[10] But, almost in the same breath, she added, "The feeling here is that we don't want special deals or special treatment for Quebec. We're very egalitarian."[11]

Bill Good, a well-known BC broadcaster, observed: "There is too much entrenched resistance here to distinct society and disbelief in politicians trying to convince them yet again that something they voted down as being wrong is right."[12] Yet six months later he stated: "Many in BC genuinely want an accommodation that allows Quebec a reasonable place in Confederation."[13]

Many have been prepared to acknowledge the enduring challenge that Quebec nationalism poses for the rest of Canada, including BC. Gordon Gibson began one of his books with the observation that the "tensions with Quebec are not going to go away on their own. They must be dealt with, one way or another."[14] Jeff Scouten, a Vancouver lawyer who inaugurated an exchange of letters with a sovereigntist counterpart in Quebec in the pages of the BC Bar Association publication *The Advocate*, argued against "the breaking of the family-like emotional bond that now ties us together as different parts of a common country. Preserving this vital bond is just as emotionally important and beyond the realm of rational persuasion for me as the goal of independence may be to you."[15] BC filmmaker Mina Shum said, "I like Quebec, I want them to stay. If it goes it will break my heart – like when a boyfriend leaves you."[16]

This has led various opinion-makers in BC to support some form of distinct society status for Quebec. The Business Council of BC argued: "It is the view of the Council that Quebec represents a distinct society within the Canadian context. We say this unequivocally. The Council supports the federal proposal to recognize this distinctiveness."[17] In a 1997 discussion paper, the Vancouver Board of Trade stated: "We recommend that the unique nature of Canada's regions, including the distinct nature of Quebec, can and should be allowed to flourish within the federation."[18] Ron Burns, a former BC and federal government civil servant and the chair of the Advisory Committee to the BC Cabinet on the Constitution from 1977 to 1982, argued: "Quebec in many important respects is distinct and it may very well be that our efforts to meet this distinction have had serious shortcomings."[19] Robert Clark, emeritus economist at the University of British Columbia and longtime member of the Progressive Conservative Party of Canada, wrote: "On the whole, I strongly favoured accepting the distinct society proposal. I felt then and even more strongly now, that it is a reasonable and essential requirement to be met if we hope to keep Quebec as an integral part of Canada."[20] The Canadian Jewish Congress, no different in this respect from a good number of other multicultural organizations, argued in a December 1997 brief to the BC Unity Panel:

> The Canadian Jewish community overwhelmingly supports the idea that Quebec must remain within Canada. Along with its traditional coalition partners, Canadian Jewish Congress has traditionally recognized that the majority of Quebec's population is francophone and that it is appropriate for Quebec to preserve, protect and promote the French language, its culture and its tradition of law ... It is the view of the National Unity Committee of the Canadian Jewish Congress that the Calgary Declaration offers a recognition formula that corresponds to the long expressed wishes of a majority of Quebecois, while addressing the concerns of a number of other provinces who want to maintain their status within the Federation.[21]

In its more temperate moments, the *Vancouver Sun* gave editorial support to the Meech Lake Accord, the Charlottetown Accord, and the Calgary Declaration.[22]

It would therefore appear that moderate BC opinion-makers are prepared to see steps taken towards the acknowledgment of Quebec's distinct character, if this is indeed the price that needs to be paid to preserve Confederation. There is a larger interest at stake that trumps any regional petulance over Quebec demands.

Others have been prepared to go a step further, recognizing that Quebec constitutes something closer to a distinct nationality within the Canadian federation. Vaughn Palmer, the *Vancouver Sun's* Victoria columnist, noted at the time of the final round of the Meech Lake negotiations, "Will English Canadians ever stop dreaming the myth of Canadian nationhood? Can they accept the inevitability of 'two nations' ... within the bosom of a federal state?"[23] Tom Berger, a former BC New Democratic Party leader and judge, observed:

> Quebec's distinctiveness ought to be recognized in the Constitution. The Civil Code gives it a distinct legal system. The French language is predominant in Quebec ... There should be special status for Quebec.[24]

According to the Public Service Alliance of Canada:

> Most Canadians recognize Quebec's status and right to self-determination. We have passed a union resolution supporting self-determination. We recognize Quebec as different. They have a different way of dealing with their things. Asymmetrical confederation – Quebec can have certain powers but English Canadians also deserve a strong national government.[25]

The BC Teachers' Federation stated:

> We recognize Quebec as the home of a nation and the right of its people to self-determination. We encourage Quebec to remain in Canada and become full partners in the constitutional process. If Quebec chooses to remain in Canada, we affirm the right as well as the legislative authority of Quebec to protect its historic roots, language and culture.[26]

Such views may well be held by only a minority in British Columbia, but they reflect a current of opinion that is rooted in something other than the politics of resentment. Pollster Angus Reid notes that there may, in fact, be a more flexible BC position vis-à-vis Quebec than the strident anti-Quebec views that have often grabbed centre stage:

The really dominant mood in BC is one of sympathy and flexibility. The characterization of BC as this hard-line province with strident views on Quebec is wrong. It represents about one-third of the province, but it's a minority that Rafe Mair and others give voice to.[27]

I think, however, that it is important to balance the presentation of this more accommodating attitude by underlining the clear opposition expressed by various BC opinion-makers to any political association with a Quebec that has decided to leave Confederation:

[Gordon Gibson] It cannot be said too strongly. Our premiers must shout it from the rooftops, for Quebec won't believe Ottawa on this: *"Sovereignty-association will not be accepted by the other provinces! Do not go down this road, for on that road lies disaster."*[28]

[Tom Berger] We are entitled to ask, once again, what does Quebec want? Sovereignty association is an attempt to have it both ways. What must be understood is that we are talking about independence ... For Quebec it must be a moment of truth, unobscured by soothing sounds from English Canada about accommodating Quebec in some absurdist confederal state.[29]

The *Vancouver Sun,* in an editorial on one of the Bloc Québécois leader Gilles Duceppe's forays to the West Coast, commented:

We're not that laid back. Our thoughts are on how to keep Quebec from ripping a hole in Canada. The only partnership that makes sense is for the provinces and territories working together to improve the union.[30]

In other words, the prospects for any formal post-separation partnership between Quebec and the rest of Canada do not look very bright. And there is frequent emphasis among BC opinion-makers, not unlike that among the BC politicians cited in the previous chapter, on the need to get away from a Quebec-centred view of Confederation to something more reflective of the larger federation. "The focus of constitutional reform can't be Quebec-centred. That's a recipe for disaster for our country. There must be a pan-Canadian approach."[31]

The Federal Government and Federal Institutions
How, then, do BC opinion-makers see the federal government and federal institutions?

For one group of opinion-makers, the problems with Canada lie in the excessive power of central institutions and the solution in a significant devolution of powers to the provinces. Gordon Gibson notes:

Forced decentralization. This is no bad thing. The basic concept here is "government closer to home" ... Decentralization has come to mean shifting of power to a lower level of government ... People want more control over their governments.[32]

He goes on to talk about a redistribution of powers that would give provincial governments paramountcy in areas that are currently under federal jurisdiction, such as fisheries, culture, science, research and development, agriculture, and pensions.[33]

Mel Smith identifies himself as having an "unabashedly BC perspective."[34] For him,

The Cabinet, Senate, Commons, and federal boards under-represent BC underlining the need for greater regional power at the centre.[35]

The deep-seated alienation that exists in the west towards the federal government – any federal government – because of the lack of meaningful regional input in national decision-making is symptomatic of outmoded and unfair existing constitutional arrangements.[36]

For Walter Hardwick, a UBC geographer and past consultant to governments, "it is time that the case for devolution of power to the provinces be made – and listened to."[37] For the Business Council of BC, "devolving federal responsibilities to the provinces would de facto lead to an easing of regional grievances and give Quebec more room to manoeuvre."[38] *BC Report* declared:

The West, while lacking the equivalent trappings of nationalism, is experiencing decentralizing tendencies nearly as profound as Quebec's. The West's growing autonomy is economic rather than political or cultural. Its main elements are the dismantling of the Liberals' hated NEP, free trade with the United States and increased trade with the Pacific Rim.[39]

Decentralization, devolution, redistribution of powers – these are the priorities of opinion-makers who espouse a more regionalized view of the country. It is fair to say that those advancing such views tend to be on the right of the political spectrum; I think it is also fair to note that, unlike in Quebec, culture plays a distinctly minor role, compared with economic interests, in providing the underpinnings for their position. The appeal of BC regionalism for such figures seems to be less to the heart than to the pocketbook.

Another group of opinion-makers simply notes BC's sense of alienation from the federal government. Tex Enemark, a Vancouver businessman and former executive assistant to federal cabinet minister Ron Basford in Ottawa and later a deputy minister in the BC government, stated: "The sad fact is that Federal ministers are seen as speaking for Ottawa in BC, not the other way around."[40] David Elkins, a UBC political scientist, writing in the early 1980s, thought that "Western alienation would decline significantly if Mr. Trudeau departed from federal politics."[41] For Miro Cernetig, the *Globe and Mail*'s Vancouver correspondent in the mid-1990s,

> As they enter what they like to call the Pacific Century, when the rising economic forces are on the western curve of their ocean's horizon, British Columbians ... want to move beyond what always has seemed – and always will seem – a simplistic myth from the east: that Canada is the product of two founding cultures.[42]

According to a *Vancouver Sun* editorial of early 1999, "the West, as British Columbians well know, broadly lags in representation in the political, administrative, and judicial institutions of Canada, and in clout in Ottawa."[43] As University of Victoria political scientist Norman Ruff ruefully notes: "Ottawa tries to demonize and marginalize the BC position. And our premiers, everyone from Vander Zalm to Clark, have been engaging in demonizing Ottawa."[44]

There is, however, a countervailing point of view to that which calls for greater decentralization of federal powers or which emphasizes BC's persistent alienation from Ottawa. A significant number of opinion-makers are quite prepared to defend the role of the federal government and federal institutions against the sirens of excessive decentralization:

> [David McPhee, director of communications for the BC Medical Association and a director of the Vancouver International Airport] Our politicians have always been more comfortable operating within the stereotype of alienated BC. And sure, there are problems with federalism that need fixing. But if a BC politician stood up today and said, "Hey, I can represent

this province without constantly resorting to attacking federalism," I think people would cheer.[45]

[Bruce Hutchison, veteran Vancouver journalist and author, writing at the time of the first Quebec referendum] How much power can national government transfer to provinces, all lusting for more?[46]

[Tom Berger] By rejecting Meech we preserved the Supreme Court as a national court and we made sure that Senate reform was not translated into nothing more than a Senate that is a repository for provincial instead of federal hacks and mediocrities. We thwarted a transfer of power to the provinces that would have undermined federal programs and institutions.[47]

[Ron Burns] What we have experienced in the last few years has been a growth of the movement toward provincial power, by no means limited to Quebec. This would, if carried further, as it now appears to be, convert Canada into a country where the central government was merely an agent of the provinces with limited authority of its own – in short a weak confederacy.[48]

[UBC economist Robert Clark] I am convinced that the overall case for a major decentralization of powers is overstated ... I am opposed to having the federal Government surrender its right to provide Old Age Security benefits or Family Allowances.[49]

The *Vancouver Sun* editorial board criticized Bill Vander Zalm's infatuation with the Quebec Liberals' radically decentralizing Allaire Report of 1991: "If Mr. Vander Zalm finds constructive the idea of reducing Ottawa to little more than a clearing house for debt and equalization payments, one can only wonder what he would consider constructive."[50] And Allan Garr, a BC broadcaster and journalist, castigated Glen Clark for lacking any "vision of Canada," and lambasted Rafe Mair, the Fraser Institute, and Gordon Gibson for their cost-benefit analysis of Confederation.[51]

There is a significant difference, then, between British Columbia and Quebec opinion-makers when it comes to attitudes towards the federal government. In Quebec, even federalist francophones – such as Claude Ryan or Alain Dubuc, the editor of *La Presse* – are strong supporters of the devolution of powers from Ottawa to Quebec.[52] By comparison, many BC politicians and commentators do not question the legitimacy of fairly extensive federal powers, even in areas such as health care or higher education that fall under provincial jurisdiction. And while well-placed BC opinion-makers press for greater devolution of powers to Victoria, at least as many others are prepared to argue the opposite point of view. BC may well be a region of Canada, but this does not mean that all of its most important opinion-makers see themselves as regionalists. On the contrary, there are many BC opinion-makers for whom the pole of country is a good deal stronger than the pole of province or region. And there are many who think of the federal government as their national government, a government with claims that trump any purely provincial ones.

British Columbia as a Distinct Region

One of the most interesting themes for a study of this kind is the *different visions of region* that characterize BC opinion-makers. Some speak to geographical characteristics of the province, some to economic, some to demographic, some to environmental, some to political, and still others to attitudinal and cultural ones. Let me present the reader with some of the more compelling examples I have come across in my research.

BC's place on the Pacific Rim figures prominently in BC government publications, such as documents produced in conjunction with the now highly controversial 1997 Asia-Pacific Economic Cooperation (APEC) summit in Vancouver that spoke of British Columbia as the "Gateway to the Pacific Century."[53]

For Thomas Hutton "not only is Vancouver emerging as an important node of the Pacific Rim urban network, it is quite visibly becoming an Asian-Pacific metropolis as a consequence of inflows of Asian capital and culture."[54] Hong Kong entrepreneurs like Michael Kan speak of BC's linkage to Hong Kong, and through it to China and Southeast Asia.[55] The well-known BC writer George Woodcock argued that the next phase of BC's history, "one of growing contact with the Asian world – will synthesize its Pacific and North American loyalties, as the loyalty to Britain implied in its name becomes a sentimental one, a matter of history rather than actuality."[56] Geographer Walter Hardwick speaks of "the cosmopolitan Asia-Pacific orientation of southwestern BC," in the process downplaying its commonalties with other parts of Canada, such as Newfoundland.[57] David Mitchell describes Vancouver as "an emerging urban node among the increasingly interdependent cities of the Pacific Rim."[58] For Lisa Birnie Hobbs, a BC journalist, British Columbians tend to view "Asia as a stop away."[59] And for writer Jerry Pethick, "the West Coast has put me in touch with a soft, allusive presence of Pacific rim influence."[60]

A sense of being on the Pacific Rim underpins the contemporary BC sense of region. It has emerged quite recently, reflecting the new-found importance that the Asia-Pacific region has come to acquire in the global political economy. Japan and more recently China have loomed much larger than before in the *imaginaire* of policy-makers in North America and Europe. A sense of geographical belonging to the Asia-Pacific region has replaced a sense of estrangement from Asia in the earlier British Columbia mind-set.

BC's economy still has a significant resource underpinning. *Vancouver Sun* journalist David Ablett highlighted BC's climate and resources in a 1977 article.[61] Almost two decades later, UBC economist Ron Shearer wrote: "Despite the remarkable aggregate growth and greatly increased complexity of the BC economy in recent decades, there is no evidence that resource extraction and processing has fallen from its central position in the economic base."[62] Increasingly, however, it is the service sector and knowledge-based industries that loom large in the equation, especially in the Lower Mainland of the province:

> In 1989 three-quarters of all employment in the province was made up of service-producing industries, reflecting a 19 per cent increase over the decade ... Vancouver's incipient role as an international financial centre is also indicative of its world city status ... The growth in the quaternary sector specializing in knowledge-based industries has brought social as well as economic changes.[63]

International connectivity and global networks are now seen to be vital parts of Vancouver's urban culture and economic development.[64] In other words, the "staples" theme plays a less important role in con-temporary thinking about the BC economy than do the information revolution or the new realities of globalization.

The changing demography of BC, in particular the heavy migration from Asia that has occurred over the past couple of decades, also shapes perceptions. This may appear a tad ironic, in light of BC's earlier rep-utation as the most anti-oriental of Canadian provinces.[65] Today, the increasingly multicultural, Asia-Pacific character of the province has become a way of emphasizing BC's distinctiveness. A *Vancouver Sun* editorial of October 1995 captures some of this:

The defining elements of British Columbia's identity stand in stark contrast to those of Quebec. We are transPacific – more than 80 per cent of the port of Vancouver's business is with Asia Pacific nations and BC suppliers account for 42% of Canada's exports to the Pacific Rim. We are transglobal and multicultural – half of BC's exports are to the US, another quarter to Japan. The second most common language spoken in this province is Chinese and it is estimated that by the turn of the century, 40 per cent of the city of Vancouver's population will be Chinese. We are mobile – only about half of our population was born here.[66]

David Mitchell notes:

Aboriginals, whites, Asians and others have built a unique multicultural society that is a world apart from the population mix of other Canadian provinces ... As Greater Vancouver leads the way, emerging as an urban node among the increasingly interdependent cities of the Pacific Rim, the energy, talent and wealth of Chinese-Canadians represent a significant resource for the province. And it's one of the key reasons BC constitutes a distinct society.[67]

For his part, novelist Douglas Coupland stresses Vancouver's easygoing tolerance.[68] And Hongkong Bank financier and SFU chancellor Milton Wong observes: "British Columbians today are building a more sophisticated form of Canadian multiculturalism, with Asian, North American and other values blending into a collective identity."[69]

There may be an element of wishful thinking in all this, a fairy tale of harmonious racial intermingling that speaks to one part of the British Columbia ethos but not to others. Unlike Australia, there has been no Pauline Hanson in the British Columbia context to openly attack the virtues of open immigration. The dominant opinion-makers in BC, largely metropolitan Vancouver–based, certainly speak the language of multiculturalism. Yet one suspects that under the surface there is some resentment of the pace at which immigration has been changing the face of British Columbia. I would refer the reader to a few of the comments from ordinary British Columbians cited in the next chapter that bear this out.

Back in 1981, Joel Garreau authored a book called *The Nine Nations of North America,* which lumped British Columbia with northern California, Oregon, and Washington in something called Ecotopia. The environmental movement has been particularly strong in BC, with organizations such as Greenpeace originating in the province and others such as the Western Canada Wilderness Committee or the David Suzuki Foundation playing an active role. Not surprisingly, therefore, there is a strong environmental subtheme to certain visions of the province, such as that of the authors of *Clayoquot: On the Wild Side:*

> The ancient temperate rainforests of the Pacific coast are ... clustered between the Pacific Ocean and the mountain ranges that line the west coast of North America ... This ... ecosystem ... achieved its present form 2,000 to 3,000 years ago ... The Douglas fir, Sitka spruce and western red cedar of Vancouver Island rank among the world's largest and longest-living plants.[70]

Or that of John Mikes of Canadian River Expeditions: "We don't have the galleries and cathedrals of Europe here. We have wilderness and we will have to find some way to preserve that or we will lose our competitive advantage."[71] As three BC social scientists have observed:

> Environmental concerns are clearly salient to a substantial number of British Columbians, hence their place on the agenda of government seems assured. Moreover, these concerns are linked to fundamental values that shape the way in which people see the political world.[72]

British Columbian opinion-makers, at least, like to fancy that their province is the most environmentally friendly in Canada.

Regarding the political dimensions of BC regionalism, *Vancouver Sun* columnist Vaughn Palmer observed at the time of the 1992 Charlottetown referendum:

> I knew BC's verdict would be unique ... British Columbians said "No" for their own reasons, reasons arising out of isolation from the central orthodoxies and profound mistrust of politicians from the other side of the Rockies.[73]

This view is echoed by others:

> [Lisa Birnie Hobbs] The Rocky Mountains and the Coastal Range provide the cut-off point, a visible barrier to the rest of the nation. Nobody is unhappy about this. In fact, distance from Ottawa with its rascals and confidence men rates highly on the local consciousness index.[74]

[Norman Ruff] I think that there's a sense that BC is a sovereign entity beyond the mountains. If you talked serious politics until very recently, apart from free trade you talked BC politics. You push a British Columbian and you ultimately find a Canadian. But in day to day life they're British Columbians and the rest of the country is essentially irrelevant.[75]

[Edward McWhinney, Simon Fraser University political scientist and future federal Liberal politician] The Quebec elite still thinks of Canada as two nations. That's a 1960 notion. I would say BC is more distinct from Quebec than Quebec is from Ontario.[76]

The one dissenting note – contrariness being something of a BC characteristic, after all – comes from UBC political scientist David Elkins, who emphasizes the similarities between BC and the rest of Canada:

BC seems to fit in with the [Canadian] majority on the most contentious issues, such as favouring free trade, opposition to constitutional reforms, and providing abortions to women who seek them ... the deep consensus on striking a balance between individual and collective responsibility – with most citizens favouring quite a lot of both kinds of responsibility – characterizes BC as well as Canada.[77]

My own perception is that British Columbia opinion-makers by and large do see their province as having a political culture all its own, although there is no clear agreement about what best characterizes it: a preoccupation with provincial/regional concerns, populism, or a give-no-quarter style of party politics.

A theme that has come to loom large in recent discussions of BC's regional distinctiveness is that of its Aboriginal peoples. There are two basic currents of thought on the question of Aboriginal land title and rights, broadly dividing those on the liberal-left from those on the centre-right of the political spectrum. For historical geographer Cole Harris,

Immigrants did not occupy a wilderness ... If we better realized that immigrant opportunities in this remarkable place have always rested, and continue to rest, on the displacement of Native peoples, we would, I think, live here more thoughtfully and much more gently.[78]

Harris and his co-editor of the journal *BC Studies*, Jean Barman, commented on the historic Supreme Court of Canada decision that greatly broadened the scope of Aboriginal title in BC: "For those who understand something of the trajectory of colonialism in BC, 11 December 1997 [*Delgamuukw* v. *BC*] was a historic day. Finally, there is reason to hope, Native/non-Native relations have been placed on a more just footing."[79] For Rebecca Bateman, also writing in *BC Studies,*

> The Delgamuukw decision has shown us that antiquated and misguided assumptions and beliefs about Aboriginal peoples can have dire consequences when held by those in positions to interpret the law and to formulate policy ... Assimilationist policies will not work any better today than they did thirty, forty, or a hundred years ago, for Native peoples will continue to assert their right not to assimilate.[80]

For University of Victoria political scientist Jim Tully, "the politics of cultural recognition is a continuation of the anti-imperialism of modern constitutionalism, and thus the expression of a genuinely post-imperial age."[81] Journalist Terry Glavin commented on the opposition to land claims settlements:

> A strange populist barbarism is sweeping the small towns of this province, and it's not grounded in reality ... There's this overwhelming public sentiment that native people are getting a free ride from the provincial government and it's the exact opposite. They've done everything they've had to do in law.[82]

On the opposite side of the issue, arguing for a much more limited recognition of Aboriginal claims, one finds views such as the following:

> [Mel Smith] *Delgamuukw* [is] one of the most audacious acts of judicial engineering in our history ... The native leadership ... must be reminded that public support for the land claims process is very much on the wane. We must deal fairly, but it must be in a balanced way, and this is a matter for governments to decide.[83]

> [University of Victoria political scientist Terry Morley] This distant and disdainful Court places the economic prosperity of BC in grave peril ... a court in faraway Ottawa, with modes of reasoning foreign to BC's sensibilities, has revived our colonial status and made itself and its subordinate judges our effective rulers.[84]

[Gordon Gibson, writing about the Nisga'a treaty] The problem of accountability is escalated because the Nisga'a government will largely be using "other peoples'" money ... A closed society is almost certainly going to be less vital and interesting than an open one, nor will it present as many opportunities to its members ... Non-aboriginal residents of Nisga'a territory will clearly not be equal to Nisga'a residents. There is a definite Charter issue here ... Indian government is a conceptual mistake.[85]

[Alma Howard of Nanaimo, the one non-specialist solicited by Attorney General Bud Smith to contribute to the 1991 *Discussion Papers on British Columbia in Confederation*] Aboriginals should have self-administration on a municipal level – on their own allocated land – including, their own social laws ... Aboriginals living outside allocated land should be treated the same as any other Canadian and subject to all Canadian laws. The aboriginal people must not be condemned to live a parasitic existence – nor should ordinary Canadians be exploited by them "working the land/resources" while the aboriginals sit back and "cash in."[86]

Well might one of BC's foremost experts on Aboriginal politics, Paul Tennant, note:

The gathering momentum of the treaty process itself has served to raise concerns among the non-Native public, and the two provincial opposition parties have found much to criticize in the process ... Aboriginal issues have reemerged as conspicuous and controversial subjects in news coverage and in political debate within BC.[87]

Within BC, therefore, Aboriginal issues often eclipse the pan-Canadian national unity debate. There is a fair degree of correlation, I would contend, between support for settlement of Aboriginal treaty claims within BC and support for recognition of Quebec's distinctiveness within Canada, just as there is a fair degree of correlation between opposition to the one and to the other. Resentment is an important feature of this opposition, a sense that Aboriginal peoples, just like Quebec nationalists, are pressing for special privileges vis-à-vis ordinary British Columbians. Chapter 4 provides further evidence to back this up.

For a long time, outside observers have been wont to think of BC as the repository of the Canadian dream. Robert Fulford, writing in 1976, saw in BC "an image of the future that isn't entirely defeated or decayed."[88] Carl Mullins, who edited a special 1992 *Maclean's* issue on the province, described BC as "the country's wake-up province – a generator of experiment, action, and ideas."[89] This is also one of the ways that BC commentators have tended to define their province's distinctiveness:

[Writer and naturalist Roderick Haig-Brown] British Columbia has the wealth, energy, and newness to become the most enlightened and humanitarian of all the provinces.[90]

[Lisa Birnie Hobbs] In BC, people tend to view history as something that happened last weekend ... Its key words are "energy" and "future." History here tends to be recent, anecdotal and fragmentary ... We generally favour the future over the past. Let Quebec say "Je me souviens." As for us, "L'avenir c'est moi."[91]

[Justine Brown] In all our eastward travels, we remembered BC as the place most tinged with *possibility* ... It is arguable that BC's identity lies precisely in this "nowhereness." This phantasmagoric coastal terrain – its mists, its watery greys, its bluegreen heights, and all its imagined limitlessness – has long given rise to dreams of utopia ... Utopia is, in my opinion, the most resonant metaphor for BC.[92]

[Novelist Jack Hodgins] There is a sense here, living at the edge of the continent, that this is also the extreme frontier of the world. Old realities can be thought of as left behind in old countries (England or Hungary or Nova Scotia or Ontario or whatever) and new realities can take their place, the realities of Lotus Eaters perhaps.[93]

[Novelist Douglas Coupland, speaking about Vancouver] We're pretty much the world's youngest city. This is our strength. We have the time and the free will to create our vision and it seems we're doing a good job of it.[94]

I would observe, however, that it is difficult to build regional identities on something as ethereal as the future. A sense of the past has usually constituted the sine qua non for most forms of regionalism (and nationalism) that, politically speaking, have ever gotten off the ground. There is something indeterminate, and perhaps ultimately undefinable, in the formulations I have just cited. And it is unclear just what kind of utopian future – be it brave new world, cyberspace region, mean-spirited El Dorado, or New Age commonwealth – the denizens of a BC society that can remake itself continuously from scratch actually have in mind. A society whose opinion-makers have not quite come to terms with its past, and in some cases even deny that it has a past, may be in a poor position to articulate a core set of social values for the future. And the political and cultural vacuum that results can easily be filled not by something positive but by something a good deal more negative, such as the rejection of any core values that are seen as having come from eastern Canada.

Another feature often noted by BC commentators is the province's sense of marginality with respect to the rest of the country:

[Historian Jean Barman] BC hovers on the edge of a continent. Mountains cut off most of the province on the east, an inhospitable environment on the north, an ocean to the west, and another nation on the south ... In the final analysis, the BC identity goes beyond economics or politics or human and spatial diversity. A certain irrationality intrudes.[95]

[Daniel Gawthrop, author of a book on the Harcourt government] British Columbia likes to think of itself as the rebel of Confederation.[96]

[Columnist Allan Fotheringham] The province, in fact, is the Canadian equivalent of Ireland – contemptuous of authority, anarchistic by nature, wetted by dew almost every single day of the year, an island unto itself because of its mountains. The province simply does not care because of the gift of nature ... This is the only province of the 10 that is dedicated to hedonism.[97]

[Peter Newman, a transplant to British Columbia towards the end of his journalistic career] Life here is somehow reminiscent of a comment made by the mad knight in Miguel de Cervantes's Don Quixote. In a rare moment of lucidity Quixote asks the reader to join him "in casting off the melancholy burden of sanity." That's it. Welcome to BC.[98]

All this tends to reinforce the image of BC, when viewed from the East, as a place where, to cite Jamie Lamb, *Vancouver Sun* Ottawa columnist in the 1980s, "the politics are Crisco flaky, the unions bold and wild, the millionaires more monied and crazy than the rest of the country."[99] BC is the home of new, unconventional social movements; a California North where new trends from neoconservatism to environmentalism will eventually come to influence the Canadian body politic.

Even the Canadian love-hate relationship with nature can take distinct forms in BC. Robin Skelton begins one of his poems with the following lines:

> The wind's in the west tonight,
> Heavy with tidal sound;
> the hush and rattle of trees,
> the indrawn breath of the shore,
> do what they must.[100]

Earle Birney, in his most celebrated poem, "David," writes:

> The peak was upthrust
> Like a fist in a frozen ocean of rock that swirled
> Into valleys the moon could be rolled in. Remotely unfurling
> Eastward the alien prairie glittered.[101]

According to Russell McDougall, "BC ha[s] always thought itself different from the rest of Canada ... The image of nature in BC literature, for example, is nurturing rather than alienating, portraying a promised land where spring, not winter, is central to imagination."[102] And for bill bissett: "There is a lot of west in my poems. The rain forest, the sound of the people's heads, and the kind of interior music that is here on the coast. And the space, the trees. And there's a lot of green in my poems, from the ferns and the pines."[103]

All these currents contribute to a sense of regional distinctiveness. On this there seems to be general agreement across the board, although in good BC fashion political commentators give it their own particular twist:

> [Tom Berger] British Columbians know their province is distinct, indeed, unique, relatively, that is, if compared to any of the other provinces. Quebecers know their province is distinct and unique absolutely.[104]

> [George Woodcock] The merit of regions conscious of their own identity, of their collective selfhood, is that they can overleap the limitations of nationality and take their own places in the broader world, as Quebec has done and British Columbia undoubtedly will do.[105]

[Pat McGeer] Canada needs a regional rejuvenation, a renewal of a partnership of equals. We have our own distinct society to promote and protect. We have our own history, embedded in our very name. We have
our own culture ... our own working language – English ... our own economy ... BC needs its own political party – the BC Party.[106]

[Gordon Gibson] The traditional regional differences of Canada based on
history and differing economies have now been exacerbated by demographic shifts, originating inside and outside of Canada. Our goal varia-
tions are more regional than ever, in a cultural sense, just as they are
being homogenized on another axis by the global economy and the
Americanization of world culture.[107]

True, Vaughn Palmer could poke fun at some of the foibles in the
BC version of distinctiveness, highlighting breach of trust allegations
against Bill Vander Zalm and serious criminal charges being laid against
one of Rita Johnston's candidates in the 1991 provincial election with
the observation, "Yep, this is what makes BC so distinct."[108] And a
decade earlier Moira Farrow, another *Vancouver Sun* reporter, challenged the very place of regionalism in BC political culture: "Regionalism will be the death of Canada. Let's trade it in for a little bit of
nationalism."[109]

Nonetheless, the prevailing sentiment among opinion-makers is that
British Columbia does constitute a region apart. Do the different elements that compose it add up to a coherent whole, a clear sense
of the BC identity or of BC's place within the Canadian ensemble?
How much of the concept of region in BC involves the imagined belly
button that Ernest Gellner talked about in his discussion of nationalism, transposed to the politics of regionalism?[110] This could be the
stuff of endless debate. And it would be a sign of a certain maturing
in British Columbian intellectual and political discourse if one saw
more debate about the actual content of a British Columbian regionalism in the future.

BC Separatism

There may be no easy agreement about the nature of BC regionalism. A good deal more problematic, however, are the claims of some
in British Columbia that BC's destiny lies in out-and-out independence from Canada. BC separatism is not a purely twentieth-century
phenomenon, to be sure. As Bruce Hutchison noted about British
Columbia's nineteenth-century settlers, "this land the [early] British

Columbians regarded almost as a sovereign land, themselves a chosen people."[111]

The sirens of BC (or occasionally western) separatism – particularly in the event that Canada breaks up as a result of Quebec's secession – have not been lacking. One of its first proponents was Doug Christie, a Victoria lawyer and the founder of a short-lived Committee for Western Independence in the mid-1970s:

> Confederation is a good thing if you live in central Canada: you have access to the resources of the West without having to do anything for the West, except to benefit from a captive market for your manufactured goods. Well, we're tired of being led down the garden path. It's time to part. And anything short of real independence is a waste of time.[112]

One of the founders of Greenpeace, Bob Hunter, tried to give the issue a more environmental slant, talking about a "Cordilleran alternative" and emphasizing the greater degree of environmental consciousness to be found in BC than elsewhere in the country as a justification for BC independence.[113] George Woodcock, the anarchist and writer, weighed in with the observation that "the people of Quebec have gained many advantages – enough to transform their society radically – by insisting on the third option, on the right to choose whether they remain in Canada. It is time the rest of us began bargaining from the position of strength which the insistence on such an option gives us."[114] A BC Tory member of Parliament, Ron Huntington, called for the establishment of a western parliament "to neutralize the east" and achieve control over its own economy and resources, and for a "council of regions" to decide policies with respect to communications, immigration, the Bank of Canada, and federal finances.[115] Bill Hamilton, a former head of the Employers' Council of BC, noted that "separatists are a small minority, but include responsible, informed people."[116]

More recent proponents of BC separatism have come from all walks of life. In early 1990, *BC Report* highlighted an Okanagan-based contractor named Fred Washburn, who was trying to kick-start a BC separatist movement: "I think BC could start the whole process of secession and other western provinces would follow. With the resources we have here (in BC), we could all become wealthy."[117] (The movement he started attracted a few hundred members, but fizzled out two years later.)[118] Mark Mosley, a Vancouver lawyer and former aide to federal cabinet minister Ron Basford, penned an op-ed piece in the

Vancouver Sun in 1991 entitled "Welcome to the Republic of Pacifica." In it, he addressed the different options BC would face in the event of Quebec's separation, underlining BC's abundant physical resources and well-educated population: "There are valid historical and social reasons why the prospect of an independent BC should not be rejected out of hand ... this choice must present the greatest opportunity for realizing our full potential and satisfying our deepest aspirations."[119] In 1994 David Mitchell, then an independent Liberal member of the BC legislature, stated that "if our Confederation is torn apart by Quebec's possible separation, we will need to recognize our citizenship, we will need to put BC first."[120] A Reform Party activist, Suan Booiman, is cited in a 1995 *Sun* article as stating that "the only solution is to leave the sinking ship and take BC out of Canada. Confederation has not been beneficial for BC."[121] In 1996 Gordon Wilson argued in a newly published book:

> On the face of it, British Columbia would do quite well as a small nation state. BC's separation from Canada, as unthinkable as that is for us all, may well be the only way we have to protect the quality of life that we have learned to love as members of Canadian society.[122]

Not to be outdone, talk show host Rafe Mair has made the argument even more boldly:

> As things now look, BC will be an independent nation inside the first decade of the next century ... an independent BC, probably calling itself Cascadia. BC, or Cascadia, will develop much closer relationships with the four adjacent American states, but will not join them politically.[123]

In some of the foregoing passages the reader will detect a sense of resentment towards central Canada and towards Quebec in particular; in others, a feeling that BC may have no option but to emulate Quebec if it comes to the breakup of Canada. In other words, support for BC separatism, when it occurs, is rooted less in a positive vision of a fully constituted BC region-state than in a negative vision of Canadian federalism or of what a post-Quebec Canada might represent. It is the separatism of people who feel that BC has little to lose by veering off on its own, not of people who think of their province as constituting a nationality apart.

There have been episodic attempts to describe the life of a separate BC/Vancouver. In 1977 *Vancouver Sun* journalist Neale Adams portrayed a province with a fluctuating BC dollar, forced to purchase patrol air-craft and a destroyer to patrol its 200-mile fishing limit, and facing continuous conflict involving the Lower Mainland, the Interior, and Vancouver Island. The NDP, the Official Opposition in this indepen-dent BC, wanted eventual reunification with Canada.[124] In 1997 *Van-couver Magazine* ran a tongue-in-cheek feature story by David Beers with the title "Vancouver Secedes." Beers described a Vancouver City-State "with its high tech salmon festivals, zero-tolerance diaper recy-cling, three dozen microbreweries and 31 types of year-round locally grown salad greens – a heaven where newly resculpted thighs can hackeysack 24 hours a day on blissfully smoke-free beaches." It was a city with Quality of Life Enforcers and twelve different flags, one for each month, with different corporate sponsors.[125]

What's sauce for the goose can also be sauce for the gander. On the subject of separation, it is therefore worth mentioning a number of proposals that have surfaced over the years for the separation of sub-regions of British Columbia from the province. In 1974 Brian Klaver, the mayor of Port Hardy on Vancouver Island, initiated a move to get the northern part of the island to join Alaska as a way of protest-ing inadequate ferry and road links to the rest of the province: "We are very dissatisfied with the provincial government, and therefore with the Canadian government. If Alaska is interested in having us join them, perhaps we'll be able to get the services we deserve."[126] In 1989 Jack Kempf, a disaffected Social Credit member of the legislature, spoke out in favour of northern separatism, arguing that northerners were "sick and tired of being told what to do by Victoria bureaucrats."[127] In 1998 Robert White-Harvey wrote an op-ed piece for the *Globe and Mail* entitled "Why Vancouver Island Should Go It Alone." He pointed out that Vancouver Island had almost five times the population of Prince Edward Island; that the island had been experiencing a steady erosion of services, economic power, and control over its destiny; and that Victoria would thereby become the true capital of a new province rather than the host city for a government controlled by Vancouver.[128]

Overall, the critics of separatism have far outweighed its supporters among BC opinion-makers – a signal difference, I would argue, between the situation in British Columbia and that in Quebec. Back in the 1970s and early 1980s, when movements for western separation were briefly getting off the ground, Marjorie Nichols, the veteran *Vancouver Sun* columnist, dismissed them as "an incipient case of virulent kook-ism."[129] She went on to observe, with reference to provincial cabinet ministers like Pat McGeer, that "the only place a separatist referendum could be guaranteed passage would be in the BC cabinet room."[130] And she praised Garde Gardom, BC's minister of intergovernmental affairs, for having repudiated separatism in a Toronto speech:

> Good for Garde Gardom ... BC's minister of intergovernmental affairs said in simple, unequivocal, and emphatic terms that the government of this province will not brook association with any separatists anywhere ... There was none of the petty whining, to which we have become so accustomed, about how the East is stealing the West's riches, about how British Columbians are going to go barefoot because of the new federal tax on natural gas.[131]

At about the same time, Jim Kinnaird, president of the BC Federation of Labour, spoke out strongly against any form of BC separatism:

> Look around and see who is talking about Western separatism the loudest. Is it working people? Is it trade unions? No. It is a bunch of two-bit, free enterprise politicians who are talking about separation. Working people in Western Canada are proud to be Canadians. We know the strength of unity, even if they don't.[132]

Anyone with knowledge of the strong support that Quebec union leaders have shown for the sovereignty cause ever since the Quiet Revolution and the emergence of the Parti Québécois cannot but note a salient difference with British Columbia. But then modern-day Quebec nationalism has had a more left-of-centre dimension to it than has BC separatism. The champions of devolution of power to provincial governments in provinces like British Columbia do not have a social democratic model of society in mind.

Three further newspaper columns from the late 1970s and early 1980s help to underline the relative thinness of support for BC-style separatism. David Ablett, editorial page editor of the *Vancouver Sun,* told a 1977 gathering of the Women's Canadian Club: "My own feeling is that in the vast majority of British Columbians there is a visceral and abiding belief in and indeed affection for Canada – whatever might be said by those who test Confederation against the standards of the counting house."[133] In a dismissive tone, Allan Fotheringham saw separatists fitting in with the cults and sects endemic to BC.[134] And Denny Boyd, a *Sun* columnist, noted in 1981 that "an Easter blessing for all of us is further confirmation that western separatism is dying, a probable victim of its own high blood pressure ... The big crowds have stopped coming to hear [Elmer] Knutson [of the Western Canada Federation] bash everyone east of the Manitoba-Ontario border."[135]

Nor were the critics lacking when the next round of separatism got going in the 1990s. For Tom Berger, "western alienation is not an issue of the same order of magnitude as Quebec independence. To equate these stale cries for political aggrandizement to Quebec's call for national independence is to magnify the one and trivialize the other."[136] According to David Beers, "there's been a lot of talk out here about separatism, about BC going it alone and doing fine, usually from the same old people. Nobody thinks everything would be fine if BC or Vancouver separates. This is a cautionary tale ... you exchange one master – Ottawa – for many others that might be less benign."[137] For Richard Harris, a Simon Fraser University economist, "BC separatists have incredibly rosy views of the future. They have experienced wealth and they see all this stuff in the paper about Quebec and Newfoundland sucking them dry. They get fed up and this is a huge part of the psychology."[138] *Vancouver Sun* columnist Peter McMartin reacted to Pat Carney's invocation of separatism during the altercation between the BC and Canadian governments regarding the overfishing of salmon by Alaska fishermen:

> Her idea of Canada seemed a grudging and artificially constructed one, rather than one that sprang from passion ... she is known in Ottawa for her passionate, almost pure laine attitude of things BC ... What is in question is her willingness to believe that the nation is greater than the sum of its parts. And that is why – if you love this country – she has to be stopped.[139]

Barbara Yaffe, another *Sun* columnist, dubbed Gordon Wilson, after a venture into Quebec where he met with sovereignty supporters, "BC's own father of (de)Confederation."[140]

So while it may well be true, as Gordon Gibson has claimed, that BC separatism is no joke,[141] his old mentor/nemesis Pierre Trudeau may well have got it right in a 1980 speech in Regina when he observed:

> The chances of Western separatism are absolutely nil ... I know something about separatism. I have been fighting it all my life. I know a separatist when I see one and I think I can distinguish the real article from the phony. Separatism is not something to be toyed with as a political tool. The real separatists mean it in dead earnest, and they fought for that, as you know, in a referendum in Quebec ... the reasons in Quebec

didn't have to do essentially with sharing of the big bucks, but with the right to live according to one's identity, to use a language.[142]

There is a qualitative difference between regional estrangement, essentially motivated by economic arguments, and the deeper well-springs of identity that underlie Quebec nationalism. Overall, as the *Sun* observed in the aftermath of Pat Carney's separatism caper, British Columbians seem quite happy to whine about getting the short end of the stick inside Confederation; only 11 percent show any inclination to take separatism seriously.[143]

A British Columbia Vision of Canada?

What, then, is the BC view of Canada that one can glean from opinion-makers in the province? The simple answer is that there is no one view.

There are those who, following in the footsteps of Duff Pattullo and W.A.C. Bennett, would like to redefine Canada as a five-region country with BC as a distinct region within it.[144] Mel Smith has probably gone furthest in developing this idea. He would like to see a five-region Canada with a new "Council of the Federation" as a permanent forum with ministerial representatives from the federal and provincial governments. This body, with one vote per government, would control appointments to the Supreme Court of Canada, appointments to federal agencies, and federal spending power in areas under provincial jurisdiction.[145] As for its benefits:

> The reforms to the central institutions of the federation would see the interests of the regions far more fully represented in national decision-making ... As to the division of powers, the substantial reforms proposed would greatly enhance the powers of the provinces who wish to avail themselves of additional powers.[146]

Rafe Mair is less given to elaborate constitutional proposals than Mel Smith, but he clearly shares the latter's antipathy towards central Canadian domination:

> We have allowed Ontario to get away with the myth that what is good for her is good for the land ... "National culture," as evidenced by the output of the CBC, the *Toronto Globe and Mail, Toronto Saturday Night,* and *Maclean's,* is really the culture of Toronto, occasionally supplemented

by politically correct, suitably cleansed snippets of Toronto's view of "outer Canada."[147]

He also expresses grave concern about the domination by Ontario of the House of Commons that would follow Quebec's departure from the federation.[148]

As we have already seen, decentralizing proposals win the support of commentators like Gordon Gibson and of business interest groups. "Mr. Gibson counsels ... a radical rethink of Confederation – one that involves a mind-boggling upgrade of power to the regions, especially BC and Alberta, and a concomitant diminution of power in Ottawa,"[149] wrote *BC Report* on the publication of one of Gibson's books. The Vancouver Board of Trade argues that "the federal government continue a measured process of withdrawal from operations that can be performed by provinces or cities or by non-government agencies."[150] The Business Council of BC argues that

> there are many areas such as mining and forestry policies, manpower training, immigration and certain aspects of environmental protection that could clearly be better handled at a more local level ... We would also contend that allocating greater powers to the provinces would enhance regional representation much more effectively (and efficiently) than through Senate reform.[151]

There are, of course, defenders of federal powers against the BC-first position that many politicians and opinion-makers have taken. Tom Berger is perhaps the most outspoken:

> The premiers speak for the provinces, not for Canada ... We in Canada believe in a public sector that helps to knit the country together through transportation and communications, linking the vast spaces of the country. We have our network of social programs, the centrepiece of which is medicare. We have our national institutions, such as the CBC. We have avoided the extremes of wealth and poverty that disfigure US society. We believe in government intervention to assuage the condition of the weak and to ensure Canadians everywhere a decent standard of living.[152]

Ron Burns criticizes the "Ottawa-bashing" that has become a basic part of provincial politics no matter what party is in power, and goes on to argue the case for a constitution in which not all provinces (for example, Quebec) are required to be of equal status.[153] For Robert Clark, "the negotiations of a revised Canadian Constitution should not be based on the assumption that every power offered to Quebec should be offered to every other province."[154] The BC Teachers' Federation advocates "a sovereign, united Canada, with a strong federal system of government." It goes on to make the case for recognizing the inherent right of First Nations peoples to self-government and a social charter.[155]

When he was still an academic, Edward McWhinney adopted a more middle-ground position, arguing that "federalism is, above all, a highly flexible governmental form, that requires pragmatism and flexibility for its successful operation."[156] For its part, the *Vancouver Sun* sees BC as embracing a new reality, "in a manner designed to stimulate regional independence and prosperity, while also enhancing the nation's collective strengths."[157]

There is thus a lively divergence among British Columbia opinion-makers about the relative roles of the federal and provincial governments. This will carry over into any future debates about remaking the federation, especially if Quebec separates, and it underlines how difficult it may prove to arrive at any unified BC position, the sine qua non of effective regional participation on the national stage.

Despite David Mitchell's claim to the contrary,[158] the fact remains that British Columbians have not played that prominent a role in advancing proposals to remake a Canada that includes Quebec. Nor have they contributed very much to thinking about how to keep the rest of Canada together in a post–Quebec separation scenario. A number of commentators note the limits of BC's engagement in things national in character. According to Jean Barman, "BC still hovers on the edge of a nation. And so too is the British Columbian's identity formed ... Ambivalence towards Canada as a whole is facilitated, perhaps made possible, by the existence of an alternative hub around which most lives willingly or unwillingly revolve."[159] UBC political scientist Richard Johnston, referring to matters constitutional, criticizes a "petulance in BC not consistent with a place that wants to pretend it's grown-up and sophisticated."[160] For Tex Enemark,

> BC's representatives in Ottawa have rarely been united, disciplined, and well led, with the result that BC's federal efforts and presence are diffuse and ineffective ... Simply put, British Columbians don't participate ... BC's loss is also the country's, because we have not contributed, except financially, to the country, to the extent we should have.[161]

And Bruce Hutchison laments a lack of leaders of calibre in BC:

> To be sure, the West has long-standing and legitimate grievances, but if it must struggle for justice why has it failed to elect leaders of any party able to argue its case convincingly, or even coherently? Why do the young and ablest Westerners avoid politics like the plague while Easterners seem to revel in it? And why can't we keep things, good and bad, in reasonable proportions?[162]

BC opinion-makers can be quite defensive in the face of criticism of their relative isolation from things Canadian – especially when it comes from the outside. I need but cite the reaction of some fairly prominent scions of the BC establishment to criticism by Pierre Trudeau, at a Liberal fund-raising dinner in 1981, of the tendency of British Columbians to dwell at the foot of mountains but never to climb them.[163] Chuck Connaghan, an industrial relations consultant, retorted, "I don't think we're out of touch with the rest of the country. I think the rest of the country is out of touch with us. There's an awareness of the country and the rest of the world. It's pretty cosmopolitan." Peter Bentley, president of Canadian Forest Products, stated that British Columbians were insulted by Trudeau's suggestion; "I think British Columbians understand Canada as well as any other Canadian understands it." And Douglas Cole, acting director of the Centre for Canadian Studies at Simon Fraser University, argued, "I doubt that BC is any more insular than the rest of Canada. I don't think [Trudeau] understands the gripes of the West. He fails to understand what lies behind them."[164]

The lady protesteth a great deal, methinks. Sooner, rather than later, we shall have to see just what role British Columbians – particularly British Columbia opinion-makers – are prepared to play in the task of nation making, not simply region making, that may face the country. Then, and only then, will we know whether British Columbians can see beyond the mountains beneath which they dwell.

Conclusion

BC opinion-makers come in different shapes and sizes. Overall, business circles and those journalists or consultants who are close to them tend to favour decentralization of federal powers and a greater regional stance for British Columbia. For their part, organized labour and more liberal-left sections of opinion – for example, in the universities, the arts, media, and multicultural communities – are friendlier to federal powers. Some of the same cleavage characterizes views with regard to Quebec's distinctiveness or to Aboriginal treaties.

One might be tempted to see something of a right-of-centre bias to BC regionalism. This would correlate rather well with the right-of-centre bias to regionalism in places like Italy, with its Lega Nord, or in the Flemish region of Belgium. It also feeds into the strongly decentralizing message that the Reform Party has been articulating over the past decade. By way of contrast, support for Quebec nationalism in the period since 1960 has tended to be more strongly associated with the centre-left of the political spectrum in that province.

Not all opinion-makers to the right of centre are avid decentralizers, however. Figures like the late *Vancouver Sun* journalist Marjorie Nichols or UBC economist Robert Clark come to mind: they were no more prepared to support a wholesale power grab by BC governments than those on the liberal-left.

Potentially, regionalism and nationalism stand in tension with one another as poles of allegiance and identity. Yet they do so in a way that is different from the situation when it comes to the adherents of rival nationalisms, for example, Québécois and Canadian. Even those BC opinion-makers with strongly regionalist inclinations are rarely advocates of BC separatism. And when they are, it is more often for negative reasons – such as an option for BC in the event of the breakup of Canada – than because of a positive belief in the virtues of an independent BC nation-state.

An overwhelming majority of BC opinion-makers would define themselves as both British Columbians and Canadians. How many of their Quebec counterparts, when asked to define their own relationship to Canada, would consider themselves both Québécois and Canadian? Quebec opinion-makers are divided right down the middle on this type of question in a way that British Columbia opinion-makers, if asked to choose between British Columbia and Canada, quite simply are not. And there is considerably less agreement among BC opinion-makers about what might constitute a distinct BC identity than there is within Quebec about the characteristics of a distinct Quebec identity. The result is a fair degree of equivocation both about the exact nature and about the overall significance of BC regionalism. BC public opinion reflects similar divisions, as we will see in Chapter 4.

4
Vox Populi: British Columbia Public Opinion and Canadian Unity
With the collaboration of Victor Armony

In this chapter, I examine how ordinary British Columbians view the question of Canadian unity and of BC's relationship to the Canadian federation. In many respects this is a more onerous task than mapping the views of BC politicians or opinion-makers, for the 4 million inhabitants of British Columbia constitute a much larger set than the dozen or so key politicians discussed in Chapter 2 or the slightly larger group of opinion-makers considered in Chapter 3.

Fortunately, however, the initial decision to embark upon this study coincided with the public hearings of the BC Unity Panel, a twenty-two-member body made up of ten elected officials, both provincial and federal, ten private citizens, and two co-chairs that toured the province in the autumn of 1997, in the aftermath of the Calgary Declaration of September 1997. The BC Unity Panel held public hearings in eleven different BC centres ranging from Fort St. John to Vancouver; held twelve focus group discussions in six communities across the province; commissioned a provincewide public opinion survey with more than 1,800 respondents; and received more than 400 written briefs from interested British Columbians. It was only after the tabling of the panel's report in February 1998 that the BC legislature debated and, in May 1998, unanimously passed the Calgary Declaration.

What follows is a three-part analysis focusing on the activities of the Unity Panel. The first part summarizes some of the findings of the public opinion survey conducted for the panel. The second part is an extensive analysis of the views of more than 250 presenters at the public hearings; it makes use of computer textual techniques to highlight key themes and patterns that emerge. The third part presents, in fairly detailed fashion, some of the arguments contained in the written briefs submitted to the panel, supplemented by statements made by members of the focus groups. The second and third parts make use of the same thematic structure that was used in Chapters 2 and 3.

If this chapter is somewhat longer than the two that precede it, it is because I believe it is particularly important to present a comprehensive reading of the views of ordinary British Columbians.

Public Opinion Survey

The Calgary Declaration was issued by the nine premiers from outside Quebec in September 1997. It set forth a number of principles for discussion: a careful balancing of (1) the equality of citizens before the law with (2) the equality of provinces; (3) acknowledgment of Canada's tradition of tolerance and compassion; (4) recognition of the place of Aboriginal peoples and cultures, of the English and French languages, and of Canada's multicultural citizenry; (5) recognition of the unique character of Quebec society with respect to the French language, culture, and civil law; (6) insistence that any powers constitutionally conferred on one province be made available to all; and (7) a call for a renewed and cooperative federalism.

The telephone survey commissioned by the BC Unity Panel was coordinated by Environics Research in mid-January 1998. It surveyed a fairly large sample of 1,812 British Columbians from around the province. Some of the questions posed echoed themes raised in the public hearings; others echoed themes raised in a number of focus groups that were convened in December 1997.[1] What were some of the survey's key findings?

Overall, 46 percent of respondents did not remember seeing, reading, or hearing anything about the Calgary Declaration, underlining the lack of interest of many ordinary British Columbians in constitutional matters. When informed of the contents of the Calgary Declaration, however, 80 percent expressed strong or some support for the Calgary Declaration, while 12 percent opposed it. Almost the same ratio of respondents supported the adoption of a resolution by the BC legislature endorsing the declaration.[2]

There was overwhelming support for the principles of equality of people and equality of provinces, with approval ratings ranging from 87 to 93 percent.[3] More striking was the fairly robust support – 62 percent of respondents, with only 36 percent disagreeing – for proposition (5), which recognized Quebec's unique character. Yet only 33 percent believed that the Calgary Declaration was extending special status to Quebec, versus 59 percent who did not.[4]

A plurality of respondents – 44 percent – felt that mentioning Aboriginal peoples as part of Canada's diversity was the right thing to have done. Twenty-four percent, however, felt that a mere mention did not go far enough in recognizing Aboriginal peoples, and 27 percent felt that it went too far.[5]

Where the operation of the federal system is concerned, 43 percent of respondents favoured shifting certain activities to the provinces, 14 percent shifting powers to Ottawa, and 27 percent keeping things as they are. Respondents tended to see immigration, environmental protection, and health as areas where the primary responsibility should be federal; and they tended to see employment training, fisheries, education, and social services as areas where the provincial government should have primary responsibility.[6]

There was a good deal of support – 81 percent of respondents – for federal equalization programs for poorer provinces, even though BC itself falls into the rich-province category. There was also strong support, however – 75 percent of respondents – for all provinces receiving the same amount of federal support on a per-capita basis for federal-provincial shared-cost programs.[7]

Seventy-eight percent of respondents agreed with the proposition that both the federal government and the provinces should set national standards in areas like health care, but there was strong opposition – 59 percent of respondents – to the establishment of any new intergovernmental body to better coordinate the activities of the two levels of government.[8]

Forty-five percent of respondents felt that BC does not receive its fair share of federal funding and transfers; 37 percent felt that it did. Far more striking was the fact that 69 percent felt that BC had less than its fair share of influence on national decisions in Canada. There was strong majority sentiment – 86-90 percent of respondents – that most federal parties are oriented towards central Canada and that BC is underrepresented in the federal House of Commons.[9]

Interestingly, 77 percent of respondents living outside Victoria and the Lower Mainland felt that their interests were ignored in provincial politics, with the sense of exclusion deepest in northern British Columbia.[10]

There was overwhelming support – 90-91 percent of respondents – for the proposition that national unity was an important issue facing Canada and that it was important to keep Quebec in Canada. But 78 percent of respondents felt that BC should develop a plan about what it should do if Quebec were to vote to separate in a future referendum.[11]

To summarize, a number of themes run through this 1998 survey of BC public opinion:

- British Columbians clearly desire to keep Canada united, if at all possible.
- British Columbians are open to recognizing Quebec's unique character where language, culture, and civil law are concerned, provided this does not take the hard and fast form of special status enshrined in the constitution.
- British Columbians are willing to support a stronger provincial role in some areas currently under federal control while maintaining a strong federal role in others.
- There is a feeling that BC may not be getting its fair share of federal expenditures in shared-cost programs.
- There is an even stronger feeling that BC is politically underrepresented at the federal level.

Computer Textual Analysis of BC Unity Panel Public Hearings*

A telephone survey on the Calgary Declaration is one thing; public hearings with the participants making their own unscripted presentations are another. This section looks more closely at the substance of the oral presentations to the public hearings of the BC Unity Panel.

In its report, the panel tended to downplay the significance of these hearings: "If [presenters] spoke clearly, they were also highly self-selected. They represented the most committed and engaged among us. They also happened to live in or relatively close proximity to one of the meeting places."[12] There is reason to believe, however, that those making oral presentations at the eleven communities where hearings were held – including Prince George, Vernon, Kelowna, Peachland, Cranbrook, Nanaimo, and Chilliwack, along with Victoria and Vancouver – were not unrepresentative of the range of views, both for and against the Calgary Declaration, for and against recognition of Quebec's unique character, to be found in the province. Moreover, these presentations by British Columbians from various walks of life have a richness of detail that is inevitably lacking from an anonymously conducted telephone survey.

The corpus of the inquiry in this section consists of the presentations made by 261 persons at eleven BC Unity Panel hearings. The

---

* This section was contributed by Victor Armony.

complete official transcripts were digitalized into a computer database of almost 250,000 words. Although the speakers did not always address the same issues or answer the same questions, their interventions constitute a fairly comprehensive representation of citizens' discourse on Canada, Quebec, and British Columbia. This makes it possible to describe and present the wide range of positions and arguments used to justify different conceptions of national and regional identity. Table 1 shows the corpus structure, by place, date, number of speakers, and total number of words.

Quebec

The panel presentations were, of course, much centred on Quebec and its current and future place within Confederation. The participants commented on the Calgary Declaration, particularly on clause 5, with its evocation of the "unique character of Quebec society." Figure 1 shows the relative frequency of the terms *Canada* (including *Canadian* and *Canadians*), *Quebec* (including *Quebecers* and *Québécois*), and *BC* (including *British Columbian* and *British Columbians*) in the presentations. Mentions of *Canada* were prevalent, but mentions of *Quebec* were also very frequent, especially when compared with mentions of *BC*.

There are 1,273 sentences in the corpus that contain the word *Quebec*. An analysis of collocations was performed on these sentences. This procedure obtains, for a given term in a corpus, a list of highly correlated words. The correlation is measured in terms of statistically

Table 1

Corpus structure of presentations made at BC Unity Panel hearings (1997)

Place	Date	Speakers	Words	Percent
Chilliwack	10 December	20	26,280	10.7
Cranbrook	4 December	17	16,796	6.8
Fort St. John	19 November	10	14,003	5.7
Kamloops	26 November	16	16,792	6.8
Kelowna	27 November	16	15,679	6.4
Nanaimo	1 December	26	27,348	11.1
Peachland	27 November	19	12,665	5.2
Prince George	25 November	18	23,651	9.6
Vancouver Eastside	16 December	33	28,066	11.4
Vancouver Westside	17 December	47	36,311	14.8
Victoria	15 December	39	27,787	11.3

Figure 1

Mentions of *Canada, Quebec,* and *BC* (per 10,000 words) in presentations made at BC Unity Panel hearings

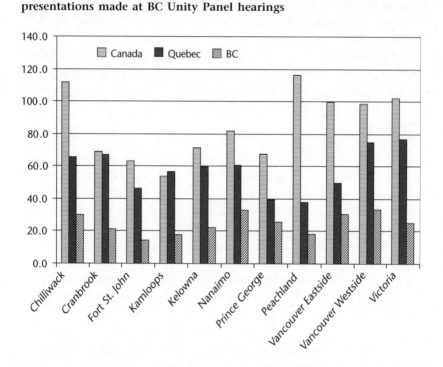

significant co-occurrence. When a word is consistently used in the same sentences where the term being analyzed occurs, the former can be said to be a "sentence collocate" of the latter. A statistical test compares the actual number of sentence collocations against the number of collocations that would be expected to occur if these collocations were random. In the case of the word *Quebec,* about thirty highly significant collocates have been identified. Figure 2 shows those words organized in terms of seven thematic clusters (collocates are in bold-face while the words that usually complete their meaning are enclosed in brackets).[13]

The first group of words that are consistently used in conjunction with the term *Quebec* refer to the rest of Canada or to English-speaking Canadians. Not surprisingly, the main theme is the tension between Quebec's demands and what the rest of Canada may or should give. Two opposite perspectives emerge clearly in the participants' discourse. One emphasizes the need to accommodate Quebec's demands:

Figure 2

Main collocates of the word *Quebec* in presentations made at BC Unity Panel hearings

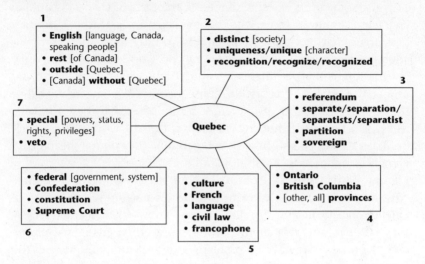

At the same time, it must persuade the *rest of Canada* that the inclusion of *Quebec* and its special interests is vital to Canada's continued existence. [Victoria]

I believe the majority of Canadians are people of such greatness of heart that reconciliation between *Quebec* and the *rest of this country* is achievable. [Vancouver Eastside]

And I really don't believe that there is a rest of Canada *without Quebec* and my Canada does include *Quebec*. [Kamloops]

The other adopts a tougher stance:

The vast majority of Canadians do not wish for a Canada *without Quebec* but due to the blatant inequality of treatment, their willingness to achieve this is not without its limits. [Victoria]

The attitude seems to be that *English Canada* must make all the changes necessary to accommodate *Quebec*. [Chilliwack]

If *Quebec* will not reason with the *rest of Canada*, then I say let *Quebec* go by, via petition. [Nanaimo]

The recognition of Quebec's distinctiveness is the theme of the second cluster of collocates. This theme is directly related to the Calgary Declaration: many speakers quote the specific clause on Quebec (clause 5) or use some of its wording to refer to the issue of Quebec's "unique character." Some of those who favour recognizing Quebec's uniqueness argue that this recognition entails nothing more than acknowledging a factual reality: "For those of you who know Quebec there is little doubt that its linguistic cultural and legal arrangements are unique in Canada" (Peachland). Consequently, "We have to recognize that Quebec is distinct, it's different" (Kamloops). For these speakers, this distinctiveness is not to be seen as a threat: "I think when Quebec talks about being distinct or being unique they do not mean being French as opposed to English" (Chilliwack).

Some participants are confused about the meaning of the terms "distinct" and "unique": "I do not know what unique character of Quebec society means any more than I know what distinct society for Quebec means" (Nanaimo). Others express their preference for one over the other: "We have no problem with the word 'unique,' but the word 'distinct' gives special powers to Quebec and we do not agree with that" (Fort St. John). Some speakers are willing to accept the term *unique,* but only if it is applied to all provinces: "We want Quebec to be recognized as its unique character but we also want all provinces to be so equally recognized" (Cranbrook). Other speakers are not interested in the semantic discussion: "Granting unique character status to Quebec will not unify Canada" (Vancouver Westside).

On the issue of "separatism" (the third cluster of collocates), the participants tend to agree that it is crucial to make sure that Quebecers are well informed about its negative consequences: "The Canadian unity forum must ensure that the vast majority of the fine and decent people of Quebec are given every detail of information in the referendum to date so that they are clear on the complete picture that could so seriously affect our future in such a devastating way" (Victoria). On the other hand, Canadians outside Quebec cannot oppose the people's democratic will: "If despite the long list of disadvantages to separation Quebec votes in a future referendum to succeed [sic], then we must accept it and then the real work, which will take years to resolve, begins" (Kamloops). This means, of course, being prepared: "We will have no choice but to address Plan B – a post-Quebec Canada if a third Quebec referendum is held and a majority favours sovereignty" (Vancouver Westside). However, not all participants proved so accommodating. Some evoked the possibility of partition: "Partition of Quebec is the answer by democratic means. The separatists will have their own country and the rest of Canadians in that province can create another province" (Chilliwack).

The fourth cluster includes references to Ontario, British Columbia, and the "other" or "all" provinces. Mentions of Ontario tend to evoke what is seen as the excessive leverage of central Canada – Ontario and Quebec – within the federal system. Thus, one speaker refers to "the fact that Ontario and Quebec seem to have a tremendous amount of power in terms of representation" (Fort St. John), while another asserts that "we have a wall around Quebec and Ontario since day one of confederation" (Peachland). Some participants express their fear that "a Canada without Quebec would be dominated by Ontario obviously and I don't think the rest of us would survive" (Kamloops). In this context, it is not surprising that "many BCers feel controlled and ignored by the two major provinces of Ontario and Quebec" (Nanaimo). Those who feel this way are not ready to make concessions: "Why should we set Quebec up on a pedestal above British Columbia" (Victoria). As another speaker puts it, "It is incomprehensible that the people of Canada, including the people of Quebec and the prime minister should think that the people of British Columbia approve of this Calgary Declaration" (Nanaimo). Some participants, however, are inclined to make common cause with Quebecers: "I think the challenges Quebec faces are shared by the other provinces and clearly are ones that BC shares" (Vancouver Westside); "To my surprise I found that we had more in common with Quebec than we had with many other provinces" (Victoria).

The fifth group of collocates refer to the distinctive aspects of Quebec society: its culture, its French-speaking majority, its tradition of civil law. These distinctive characteristics are strongly embedded in Quebec's collective identity: "They tend to identify themselves first with Quebec and their attachment to Canada is built upon this sense of a distinctly francophone society" (Cranbrook). Several speakers are aware of the need to protect Quebec's distinctive character, especially the French language: "Many francophones in Quebec feel a deep and understandable concern to protect their French language and culture from the pervasive influence of the English language of other Canadians as well as Americans" (Vancouver Westside); "We have to solve the legitimate concerns of Quebec for respecting their language and culture" (Victoria); "I think the only useful clause in that framework is that one that deals with Quebec and suggests that Quebec should have powers to, you know, guarantee its language and culture" (Chilliwack); "But I do see the need for Quebec being protected for what happens within its own boundaries in regards to its language and culture" (Fort St. John). Not every participant, however, recognizes the need for Quebec to further support and develop its distinctive character. For some, this distinctiveness is already excessive: "Quebec has more than equality already. What else would you call it when Quebec has its own civil law code, control over income tax collection, a separate public pension, and laws asserting the primacy of the French language, plus a host of propounding [sic] parochially cultural institutions" (Nanaimo).

The last two collocate groups refer to the federal and constitutional structure and to the special powers, status, or privileges – particularly a right of veto – that recognition of Quebec's unique character might entail. Regarding the federal system, several speakers point out that Quebec is not the only province with cause for complaint about the central government: "I think first of all the federal government is going to have to finally admit that they have to start delegating a lot more power to the provinces in order to keep a lot of the people happier, whether you're in British Columbia or in Quebec" (Cranbrook). In this respect, British Columbians can even identify with some of Quebec's demands for greater autonomy.

Other than acknowledging the need for a reform of the federal regime, however, most speakers who address the question of "special status" for Quebec within Confederation are adamant about not being ready to yield any power or privilege that could threaten provincial equality: "Allowing Quebec an exclusive veto or distinct society recognition will provide the province of Quebec with legal powers greater than those that would be available to any other province" (Vancouver Westside); "Vive Quebec and God bless them but I don't see them in that they should have any special privileges" (Kelowna); "Like the neverendum referendums of Quebec, we have the neverendum attempts to entrench in the body of our constitution special status for Quebec" (Nanaimo); "And what the federal government in Quebec want is for one province to be French and the other nine to be bilingual and no matter how you slice it or present it or flowery phrases you put around it, that bottom line is unacceptable" (Chilliwack); "Assigning a special role to only Quebec will be a victory for Quebec separatists" (Vancouver Westside).

Granting special constitutional recognition to Quebec's distinctiveness is seen by some speakers as being especially unacceptable to western Canada: "Either we give special status to Quebec, unique character, without exacting anything in return, thus creating a nation within a nation and ignoring the west's real need for political reform – what Meech and Charlottetown attempted to do but failed" (Vancouver Eastside). Certain participants believe that Quebec already holds too much power: "For one thing during the 40 years that I've been living in Canada, I've really never known a federal government not controlled by a francophone prime minister, backed by a large number of MP's from Quebec whose francophone population is some 22 percent of Canada's total" (Victoria).

The Federal Government and Federal Institutions

Many participants at the Unity Panel hearings expressed views about the federal government. All sentences that include a reference to the federal government, system, or institutions were retrieved and classified in terms of six categories, each of which articulates a clear preference:

1 The federal government should not be weakened.
2 The federal government should respect provincial jurisdiction.
3 The federal system should be renewed.
4 BC should have a stronger voice in Ottawa.
5 Canada should be regionalized.
6 Quebec's influence in Ottawa should be reduced.

Although it is difficult to assess which of these views would garner the greatest support, it is worth noting that overall at the public hearings, the premise that the federal government should not be weakened was at least as strongly held as the opposite position, namely that the federal government should devolve further powers to the provinces.

The Federal Government Should Not Be Weakened

But I want to see a strong federal presence with national standards. [Chilliwack]

If anything, the federal government should hold onto the powers it has in order to see that we are one country, that I can go to Newfoundland if I want and know that I'm going to have a reasonably similar lifestyle with reasonably similar rights and can expect reasonably similar services from my government. [Kamloops]

Obviously, foreign affairs, defense, justice system, and immigration should be federal responsibilities and I believe it was a mistake on the previous federal government's part to give that responsibility to Quebec cuz that is not a rightful provincial responsibility. [Kelowna]

The thought that living without the protection of the federal government umbrella and relying only on local political leaders is cause for some consternation. [Nanaimo]

I was opposed both to Meech and to Charlottetown primarily because I saw them as inordinately weakening the federal government. [Vancouver Westside]

Two, I affirm the unity of Canada and the importance of a strong central federal government in opposition to those who see an easy solution to our present problems in the devolution of powers to the provinces. [Vancouver Westside]

I think what we need to do is look at those things that are common in our struggle within this confederation, and all provincial premiers together with the federal government [need to work] at a restructuring of Canada which is sensitive to provincial needs but is also very sensitive to the need for a strong Canada and strong central government. [Vancouver Westside]

The federal government's role is de-emphasized and downplayed. [Vancouver Westside]

If provincial premiers are allowed to continue eroding away federal powers, we may as well kiss any hope of approaching equity goodbye. [Vancouver Westside]

A federal government role is required in preserving the unity of Canada. [Vancouver Westside]

What I am also concerned about is [that] the federal government is giving up practically every bit of authority that it has. [Victoria]

We need to reform the Senate and we need to strengthen the federal government. [Victoria]

The federal state is far too weak and perhaps the national program and the standards around them, could be one vehicle to strengthen that sense of statehood. [Victoria]

The Federal Government Should Respect Provincial Jurisdiction

A fair and just devolution of federal powers is required. [Chilliwack]

The latest example is the federal government trying to get control of property, rights and provinces, firearms legislation; there are four provinces right now taking the federal government to court arguing with them over who has jurisdiction; the provinces don't want to give up that jurisdiction; the federal government is making efforts to seize it from the provinces. [Cranbrook]

Provincial sovereignty does not arise in the province of British Columbia because of language or culture; it's because of the usurping of provincial jurisdiction that's been going on by the federal government. [Cranbrook]

The Liberal and Conservative party vision, federally speaking, envisions more and more provincial jurisdiction being usurped by the federal government. [Cranbrook]

We've got to take the power back to the provincial governments to look after their own situation and get that Ottawa crap out of here. [Kamloops]

They've succeeded and given it all to Ottawa, and the only province that's got any guts to fight the constitutional rights is Quebec. [Kamloops]

And I think to some extent to get rid of the duplications federally and provincially we need to cut the umbilical cord so that the provinces like British Columbia and Quebec can exercise their rights in a rightful manner and be a rightful partner in confederation and also same thing provinces need to give more rights to municipalities and recognize them as a legitimate government level. [Kelowna]

Don't beat on Quebec because they're fighting like crazy; they get out from under an oppressive and tyrannical regime of federal government which doesn't even exist in this country because it is not constitutionally federated by the people in a sovereign state. [Nanaimo]

If our federal government respected the diversity and equality of each province there would be more unity than there is now. [Vancouver Westside]

I don't think that federal governments should be in the culture business. [Victoria]

The Federal System Should Be Renewed

At the same time we must look to realign federal and provincial powers in the light of the constitution, so that provinces have the possibility of expressing their own uniqueness. [Chilliwack]

Our future must be more democratic with a federal government that shows initiative, leadership, and vision from Quebec to the Yukon to British Columbia. [Chilliwack]

It must simply be underlined that the people of Canada have often and clearly expressed their wishes and the fact that these reforms have not been brought has seriously undermined the confidence of many people in all provinces, the confidence they have in their federal government. [Chilliwack]

Any discussions regarding a renewed Canadian federalism must be undertaken in a manner which does not derogate from Aboriginal and treaty rights and jurisdictions of the Aboriginal peoples of Canada. [Cranbrook]

There needs to be a balance between federal, provincial, and municipal responsibilities. [Kelowna]

After all, what is federalism if it isn't the presence of countervailing roles and the division of powers among all levels of government and the general citizenry. [Vancouver Westside]

In conclusion, what I would like to say, is that I see no inherent reason why we cannot have a strong federal government and a stronger role for the provinces. [Victoria]

The policy discussion that we need, the national policy discussion, whether Quebec is in or out, what we are looking for is a new framework for a renewed federalism. [Victoria]

BC Should Have a Stronger Voice in Ottawa

But I'm getting a little tired, I've sent the politician to Ottawa and he gets ignored. [Cranbrook]

But a federal system is not supposed to be a tyranny of the majority. [Cranbrook]

And even when, if you add up all the votes from west of Manitoba, we don't have enough votes to really say we have any representation in Ottawa at all. [Prince George]

On any federal election night the new government of Canada and the balance of powers have been determined before the polls even close in British Columbia. [Nanaimo]

The election of senators within this new framework would give voters a more personal sense of projecting British Columbia's interests in Ottawa as well as greater participation in national affairs. [Victoria]

Canada Should Be Regionalized

This does not preclude cooperative federalism in a flexible federal system to accommodate the diversity of the realities of Canada's regions and sustain a national citizenship based on entitlements to social programs. [Chilliwack]

It means an electoral system that sends representation from each region of our country to our federal government to allow decisions to be made in a democratic fashion. [Nanaimo]

I believe there should be more regional government and a federal system where there is regional representation as well as a percentage of seats in government based on the popular vote. [Vancouver Westside]

We should rationalize the country into five or six federal regions. [Victoria]

Quebec's Influence in Ottawa Should Be Reduced

What's happening now is that I think the federal government, I know the federal government is promoting biculturalism and this is a great divisive aspect of what's happening to our country right now. [Chilliwack]

The capital at Ottawa has become Ottawa-Hull and too much under the direct influence of Quebecers. [Nanaimo]

Quebec has become the standard against which program and funding decisions are assessed within the federal system. [Vancouver Westside]

We have a federal public service where appointment and promotion is based on language requirements rather than merit or demonstrated competence. [Vancouver Westside]

British Columbia as a Distinct Region

Perhaps because the Calgary Declaration focused to a significant degree on Quebec's place in Confederation, few of the references to BC (629 in the whole corpus) by presenters at the public hearings are associated with a description of what BC actually *is*. Other than using the cliché about BC as the "fastest growing, most dynamic province in the country" or evoking its beauty and enjoyable lifestyle ("Every time I say that I think of Stephen Leacock's phrase; he says, the only thing better than a visit to British Columbia is to have been born here and I think he was right" [Victoria]), participants did not define BC's particular identity.

The notion that Canada is composed of five regions, one of which is British Columbia, surfaces in several hearings, although not especially frequently:

The current House of Commons with its proportional representation does not provide equitable opportunity for the various regions of the country to be heard and to influence national legislation. A Senate with equal representation from each of Canada's five or six regions, one of which is BC, and a Senate with real authority over matters of national importance is the one way of providing a more effective balance of power in our country. [Chilliwack]

The Supreme Court should be better reached and it should, there should be better regional representation. One idea to keep Canada united would be to restructure by dividing into five regions – the Atlantic provinces, Quebec, Ontario, combine Manitoba, Saskatchewan, Alberta, and then British Columbia. [Nanaimo]

Some general principles to guide fundamental reformation of Canadian institutions are equality between the regions. The federal Liberals finally got it right when they divided Canada into five regions: Ontario, Quebec, the Maritimes, the West, and BC. Of course they did not include the north which I think was a terrible mistake. This regional division must provide the basis for dividing political power. [Vancouver Eastside]

It is our belief that a second sober look at legislation for the protection of regional interests can best be achieved if the five regions are equally represented in the Senate. [Vancouver Westside]

I propose the abolition of provincial governments and the establishment of a second level of government based on the reality of the 21st century, that there be five regions, the Atlantic, the Quebec, the Ontario, the Prairie, and the Pacific region and that these regions be given the right to protect language and culture. [Victoria]

BC Separatism

The possibility of an independent British Columbia is raised on a few occasions only, and almost exclusively to warn against it:

During some of the recent media coverage of Senator Carney's vocal ruminations about the possibility of British Columbia separation, I think many of us felt a twinge of the extraordinary feeling of loss that would overcome us if this country was anything less than whole. For many of us I believe it was the first time that we really appreciated the sense of apprehension that our fellow Canadians in Quebec must live with every day. [Chilliwack]

I don't like to hear anyone say we're going to separate BC – like we're going to [put] a border between Alberta and BC when tourists get heavy and we can't get into a parking space. But no, there's no province in this country of ours [that] has the right to break up the country. [Cranbrook]

But I think [the intergovernmental affairs minister Stéphane Dion] also did a good job when he said to Pat Carney when she was making noises about maybe Quebec or BC should separate as well. That's just totally irresponsible. [Fort St. John]

In the event of a disintegration of Canada we may expect very compelling voices to be heard on both sides of the border, urging the assimilation of the economically strongest parts of our country into the United States. Ontario has industry and commerce, Alberta has oil, and BC has water, minerals, and lumber. Annexation of BC to the US would give a direct to land connection between Alaska and the US heartland. [Kamloops]

An article in the *Vancouver Sun* last fall said that the MLA Gordon Wilson had completed his report to Premier Glen Clark on the constitutional feasibility of BC separating and it was possible. Another section of this article cited a local politician as saying that there are plenty of leaders in this province capable of running this country, meaning a separatist British Columbia. Just who are these leaders and where are they? Why do they not run in federal and provincial elections if they're so capable? [Nanaimo]

I'm a strong federalist and I don't ever see separation of any provinces of this country from this country, including Quebec and as far as British Columbia and other provinces. I think it's just empty talk. [Prince George]

When we hear Glen Clark pretending to speak for British Columbians by saying that unless more attention is paid to British Columbia, we also might consider separating. He's not speaking for me or anyone I know. [Vancouver Westside]

A British Columbia Vision of Canada?
The discussion of Canada at the panel's public hearings focused to a large extent on the relationship between Canada and Quebec, rather than between Canada and British Columbia. There are 1,288 sentences in the corpus which contain the word *Canada*. Of these, 451 (35 percent) include an explicit mention of Quebec or the French-speaking people. In the cases in this corpus where the speakers refer exclusively to Canada, four main themes emerge: unity, diversity, equality, and national pride.

Unity

Somewhere during this evolution all provinces must become, must come to a consensus that Canada as a nation is indivisible. [Chilliwack]

Now no one has the right to break up Canada. [Cranbrook]

We must contend with what is a very real threat of the disintegration of Canada. [Kamloops]

And I don't believe in hyphenating Canadians and I think that pushing multiculturalism has created hyphenated Canadians which has been a source of division, not unity in Canada. [Kelowna]

I have a strong commitment to Canada and to Canadian unity. [Nanaimo]

I'm a Canadian by choice and I would like to see Canada remain united. [Peachland]

And I believe that the key to unity in Canada is to change the federal system. [Prince George]

I certainly would like to see Canada stay together and we together hand over our country to our next and future generations. [Vancouver Eastside]

Canada is so much more than the sum of its parts. [Vancouver Westside]

The majority of the people are for a united Canada, so am I. [Victoria]

Diversity

I believe also that multiculturalism is a integral part of the fabric that makes up Canada but it must not be at the expense of either the First Nations' Heritage or the two official language communities' heritage. [Chilliwack]

Regional differences exist and they're a fact of life throughout Canada. [Chilliwack]

Consequently the legislatures and governments of each province have a role to protect and develop the unique character of each province within Canada. [Cranbrook]

There are distinct societies all across Canada and in Alberta there is Ukrainian. [Peachland]

Everybody here seems to agree that Canada is a multicultural society. [Prince George]

I believe hyphenated Canadians will exist as long as Canada does. [Vancouver Eastside]

We accept that each province, each cultural community in Canada has its own way of being Canadian. [Vancouver Westside]

Equality

There are no basic rights or privileges that depend on geography, ethnicity, or anything other than being a citizen of Canada. [Chilliwack]

Prime Minister Chrétien declared that all provinces and individuals in Canada were already equal. [Cranbrook]

Equality of provinces and equality of powers as a basis for the unity of Canada. [Nanaimo]

The resolutions of our unity problems will never be solved unless we structure a Canada that treats people equally. [Vancouver Eastside]

I think the vision of an equal Canada with equal citizens is a good vision to fight a separatist vision with. [Vancouver Eastside]

There is only one status of any province in Canada, either you are a province with all the constitutional rights it entails or you are not. [Vancouver Westside]

I believe in ten equal provinces in a confederation called Canada. [Victoria]

Pride

I have great love for all Canadians because ladies and gentlemen we all know that Canada our country is the finest country in the world and we're allowing this to happen to my country. [Fort St. John]

And I'd like to tell this panel, right off the top, that I think Canada is the greatest nation in the world, that I am privileged to be a Canadian and I find it difficult, very difficult, to accept people who would detract from the quality of our nation and our civilization. [Kamloops]

We are proud of Canada not because we are one of the largest countries, but because we do consist of such extensive diverse origins now being able to reason together for the benefit of all. [Kelowna]

We're proud of Canada. [Cranbrook]

If anyone asked in what area of the world they would chose to live, Canada must be their first choice. [Peachland]

I love Canada, I think Canada should stay together, I applaud you all for listening to us and I'm glad that someone started something so we can have our voice heard. [Prince George]

Canada is the best country in the world in which to live. [Vancouver Eastside]

To close, I believe Canada is the greatest country on the planet and so do a lot of other people. [Vancouver Westside]

Conclusion

Overall, then, the public hearings provided a useful forum for concerned British Columbians to present their views on a wide range of issues pertaining to Canadian unity. Not surprisingly, most were opposed to Quebec separation; the few who addressed the issue of BC separatism were even more adamantly opposed to it. One finds a variety of views expressed on Quebec, on federal-provincial relations, and on the relative powers of the different levels of government. As for a specifically British Columbian vision of Canada, it may well be that the values of unity, diversity, equality, and pride that the foregoing quotations highlight are values that would be equally prevalent at similar public hearings in other parts of Canada. In other words, where the Canadian dimension is concerned, British Columbians may not be all that different from other Canadians – or, more correctly, from other English-speaking Canadians.

Written Briefs to the BC Unity Panel

There is one more type of analysis worth undertaking to probe BC public opinion regarding Canadian unity. It involves sifting through the written briefs to the Unity Panel and supplementing the results with some of the statements made by participants in the twelve focus groups that the panel convened during the first week of December 1997.

More than 400 written briefs were submitted to the Unity Panel. From the files compiled by the panel, I selected for further scrutiny about 30 percent of these briefs, some 125 in all. I took care to ensure that they were not simply written versions of oral presentations made at the public hearings, and that they reflected the diversity of BC views on the various questions before the panel. Some of the briefs contained one or two short, sometimes handwritten, paragraphs, in favour of or against the Calgary Declaration; others were fairly elaborate word-processed statements of six to eight pages.

To provide as comprehensive an overview of BC public opinion as possible, it also proved useful in a few cases to supplement citations from these briefs with direct quotations from the randomly chosen sample of participants in the twelve focus groups. The topics at these focus group sessions conducted by Environics Research "included general issues of concern to British Columbians, including provincial and national issues, BC's position in Canada, federal-provincial roles and responsibilities, and responses to the Calgary Declaration"[14] – in other words, some of the very themes that are the focus of this study.

Quebec
A good deal of passion surrounded the question of the recognition of Quebec or Aboriginal peoples as somehow different from other Canadians. Many of those who opposed the Calgary Declaration did so precisely on these grounds:

> I feel that the time has come to recognize only one culture in Canada, and that is Canadian culture ... How can everyone be treated equally if every small minority is given special rights? We should no longer be settling land claims with Canada's aboriginal people, and they should not be given self government, or tax breaks and treaty money just because of the colour of their skin. Quebec should not be granted distinct society status or special language laws. These are discriminatory practices that do little more than perpetuate racism and discrimination. [J.K., Mackenzie][15]

> It is time we put the Quebec issue to rest, we are one country with 10 provinces and the territories, we are not upper and lower Canada, we are

not a Canada with two founding nations. We are one Canada, occupied by Canadian citizens, not prefix-Canadians. [P.S., North Vancouver]

NO special status for Quebec or any other province, including no recognition of *distinct, unique* or anything that can be construed to make one province different from any other. [J.T., Cobble Hill]

We must stop being hyphenated Canadians. [L.C., Prince George]

For some hard-liners who wrote to the Unity Panel, the sooner Quebec left Confederation the better:

I've had enough. The best thing for all is to cut Quebec out of Canada and let them have their pure little country ... I can only hope it happens soon so the rest of us can get on with more important thing [sic] than "wooing Quebec." [M.S., Vancouver]

When they finally stop snivelling to and blackmailing the rest of us and decide to leave – give them all the help we can. Lend machines to print their own money, passports, schoolbooks, healthcare cards, auto contracts, all that sort of stuff. Make sure they have interpreters at all border crossings so that they can understand the new immigration policy which requires they speak English & have a job waiting (2 years at least) before they enter Canada. Be patient with their new civil aeronautics set-up & their own air line companies – explain that English is spoken world-wide: it's called courtesy, they may have a problem understanding that word. [C.C., Mission]

I do not believe in unity at any cost and the cost has been far too high for at least a decade! Sovereignty for Quebec will lead to liberation for occupied Canada. I believe that I will live to see this accomplished. [D.H., Victoria]

The majority of people I talked to felt strongly that the association with Quebec has been detrimental to the welfare of this country and the only solution is to encourage the province to leave – the sooner the better. Allow me please to quote a lady, who one day called a radio talk show I was listening to at that moment: "When I hear about Quebec," the lady said, "I'm scared. I'm scared that they won't separate." I regret to inform you that this is exactly the same feeling I presently have. [J.B., Vancouver]

I consider that many of the acts of the Quebec government – particularly their seeming punitive actions against English and anglophones – and many of the special arrangements with the federal government – on taxes, immigration, and pensions, for instance – are already too unbalanced for an equitable partnership. If the people of Quebec (as opposed to the "Quebec people," a concept seemingly popular there, and reminiscent of *Ein Volk, ein Reich, ein Fuhrer* – quite apropos, considering the history of Quebec nationalism) clearly want to become their own country, then I can see no reason to stand in their way. However, again as everyone who has ever been divorced knows, this kind of separation is seldom friendly, and often acrimonious ... I see "Plan B" as being the only viable option, if the people of Quebec vote, by the supermajority generally required for constitutional change, on an unambiguous question of separation. [H.C., Vancouver]

If Quebec separates from Canada, then they will be forced to allow areas of Quebec which want to separate from Quebec to do so. [B.H., (no city)]

Others who wrote briefs took a quite different position:

The question is not whether Quebec is a distinct society, the challenge is to offer all provinces, including Quebec, a strong national vision of a distinctly Canadian society that transcends mere regional, ethnic, political and – yes – even economic interests. [E.B., North Vancouver]

For me, Canada includes Quebec, period. A Canada without Quebec is *not* Canada. I have felt very proud of my fellow Canadians that we were all big enough of heart to contain within our borders, under one flag, people of such diverse cultures and origins ... I don't see much hope for unity unless the federal camp and all the other provinces reach out to Quebec with genuine concern, with an open heart. [N.J., Maple Ridge]

I have no problem with the term "distinct society" which has been horribly bandied about. [N.D., Vernon]

With respect to Quebec, we must recognize that they are one of the founding peoples of our nation ... Let's not fool ourselves, they do have a *distinct* culture which differs from anything found in the rest of Canada with the exception of Newfoundland. Their history extends back over 450 years. They speak a different language and their legal system is based on civil law rather than common law. [B.G., Enderby]

All who have visited Quebec immediately recognize that it is unique. That doesn't equate with "better," nor should it ... Canada's 30 million population cannot afford to lose a quarter, and very much likely the Maritimes to the US within 15 years. Much anti-French sentiment has an inflated opinion of Canada's world importance. [G.M., Vernon]

I want Quebec to stay in Confederation, because I believe we are stronger for our diversity. [C.G., (no city)]

The real problem for francophone Quebec has nothing to do with "respect" or "protecting and developing the unique character of Quebec society," but the rapid decline of the proportion that the francophone population bears to the total of the Canadian population. This has fallen from nearly 50% at Confederation to 33% in 1941 to 23.5% in 1996. As my friend the late Léon Dion said to me bitterly some years ago: "My great grandchildren will speak only English." The francophone population justifiably fears extinction. A majority of them hope, without great conviction, that independence of Quebec will at least postpone it. No amount of constitutional tinkering or comforting assurances that the rest of Canada really do love them addresses the problem. [J.N., Vancouver]

It is also worth recording a few of the statements on Aboriginal matters, since the views expressed on this subject, as was suggested in Chapter 3, usually overlapped with views towards Quebec:

Proposed Nisga Blueprint. I am completely opposed to any sort of agreement that distinguishes between Canadians in any way ... The best thing that we can do for future generations of Canadians is to end the current government driven, politically correct attempt to right perceived past inequities and get the native population into the mainstream of today's Canadian society. This blueprint promotes just the opposite ... There is nothing wrong with the country in its current state except that we waste far too much time and money on the issue of Quebec separation and national unity ... We should stop subsidizing and catering to them ... we in the west have put up with this continual whining for far too long. [P.O., Langley]

Subject: Nisga'a Land Claims. Canadians rejected special status for anyone or any group of people at the Charlottetown Accord. But our politicians are still not listening or paying attention to our voice and our [sic] proceeding to divide the country along racial and cultural lines. All treaty claims should be stopped immediately, we do not need or want another form of government in this country. [J.P., Delta]

I do not consider the financial demands of the Native population or the cost of official Bilingualism and Multiculturalism to be a gift. Instead of creating harmony and unity, official Bilingualism and Multiculturalism have created a divisiveness and hostility that is detrimental to Canadian unity. [S., Vernon]

And on the other side:

The principles to keeping any partnership working are simple: Majorities must be sensitive to the needs of minorities. No group should seek advantage at the expense of others. Federations work by creating mutual benefit ... Our common ground with native people is a mutual desire for better lives. [C.O., Rossland]

The aboriginal peoples were here before all of us. I think they deserve just as many rights and, if they want to govern their own cultures and such, if Quebec has the rights, I think they should get the rights based on seniority.[16] [Surrey]

The Federal Government and Federal Institutions

If one looks at ordinary British Columbians' views of the federal system and BC's place within it, the polarization is quite striking. Let me begin with a number of views favouring greater provincial power:

To have a federal government that is not elected by proportional representation confers far too much clout on Ontario and Quebec, in particular Quebec and is thus not representative of the needs or aspirations of BC. There should be no cooperation with the Federal government until they return to BC all tax revenue raised in BC. [P.W., Victoria]

I feel as if we're too far away. We're left out. You can see it ... If they need stuff in Ontario or Toronto, they seem to get it a lot quicker than here. [Campbell River]

We don't have any real clout I guess, yeah clout in Ottawa, and they just traditionally they seem to forget about us and our concerns until there's a crisis, and then they try to make us happy for a little while.[17] [Surrey]

The structure of Canada needs to be changed – decentralized into something resembling Switzerland. Federal government authority should be limited, perhaps to Defence, Currency, the Legal system, and international affairs. Taxation to be collected by the Provinces and a portion sent to the Federal government. Health and education in particular should be Provincial jurisdiction. [J.T., West Vancouver]

British Columbia must have fair participation in government. Central Canada should not have all the control. [No name, no city]

Defense product procurement and spending should be based on true competitive bidding ... Representation on Federal Boards and Commissions should be proportionate to population ... British Columbia should obtain complete control over (a) Immigration, (b) Fisheries ... Civil Service in Hull/Ottawa should be greatly reduced and wherever possible, positions transferred to provinces. [J.T., Cobble Hill]

Without revision of our federal system and the re-balancing of present federal/provincial powers, continued unity can not be assured. We refer to such things as the necessity of a true "triple E" senate if the equality of the provinces is to become a reality, and to the fact that without a re-balancing of federal/provincial powers the legitimate aspirations of both Quebec and the West cannot be satisfied. [A. and A., Horsefly]

I would not object to the provinces having more say, if it were by mutual agreement ... The civil service in Ottawa desperately needs to be drastically cut before it strangles the ability to do business in the rest of the country. [J.S., Vancouver]

On the other side of the question were strong representations in support of the primacy of the federal government:

Downloading more federal jurisdiction onto the provinces would be a mistake, as it weakens our country by turning it into a number of competing little fiefdoms, as in the case of Yugoslavia. [B.E., Victoria]

The "Balkanization" of Canada scares me silly. I fear we are growing further apart, not coming together. [C.G., (no city)]

Assumption by provinces of responsibility in areas of importance to them, e.g. immigration and fisheries, would create enormous problems as does the partial control of immigration by Quebec ... The effectiveness of the present federal government in these areas is not high. But this is an argument for a more effective and stronger federal government, not a weaker one. Would you want environmental protection to be in the hands of Ralph Klein? [J.N., Vancouver]

Canadian unity – if ever there existed such a notion – is threatened not only by Quebec separatists, but also by such elements as BC secessionists, Western malcontents, Maritimers; every citizen who has been seduced by generations of provincial politicians who believe that getting elected to provincial legislatures requires continuous bashing of the central Government, federal institutions and any policy that does not originate in their own, respective bailiwick. [C.G., (no city)]

In my view, we will be more successful and prosperous as one strong and unified country, than as a group of provinces, each struggling with a federal government. We have little enough clout as one country; as separate provincial entities we would each have next to none. [J.K., Qualicum Beach]

It is my belief that Meech Lake I and II and the Charlottetown Accord were basically "power grabs" by the provinces under the pretext and guise of the "Unity Issue." I absolutely do not wish to see this happen again. I do not wish to see the cherished principles of "accessibility, universality, comprehensiveness" sacrificed to provincial subrogation. The only way to have national standards in every sphere (health care, education, social assistance, pensions, cultural rights) is to have them federally imposed (albeit after negotiation with the provinces). [S.K., Vancouver]

Fewer powers to the other provinces and a strengthening of the federal government for the rest of us. [R.N., Victoria]

The present constitutional disarray of Canada is often presented as being evidence of the need for the decentralization of the country. It is important to recognize that, contrary to accepted wisdom on this point, Canada is currently a very highly decentralized federal system; indeed, it may be the case study of how decentralized a system of government can become and still survive. [R.B., Vancouver]

I was born and raised in Manitoba, worked for some years in Ontario and have now lived in British Columbia for over forty years. I am not "Manitoban," "Ontarian" nor "British Columbian." My nationality is

CANADIAN. It is my BIRTHRIGHT ... It seems to me that "Fed-bashing" is a very selfish practice that tends to affect the opinions of unwary citizens and ultimately feeds on itself. [W.P., West Vancouver]

On the subject of Federal vs. Provincial powers: If you were to poll the general population of Canada, I believe that you would find majority support for a strong Federal government, with enforceable *National Standards* for education, health care, social welfare, contributory pensions, etc. These are unifying issues that help to bind this country together. Recently there has been far too much emphasis on tearing the country apart, by demands from the Provinces for control over a wide range of programs that properly belong under Federal government jurisdiction. [R.B., Victoria]

In an effort to meet the demands of Quebec and some other provinces for more autonomy ... there has been a concerted move in recent years to devolve more federal authority to provincial level ... This raises a concern about going too far and leaving the federal government weak and ineffective in handling its national responsibilities ... *In any realignment of responsibilities with the provinces, the powers left to the federal government should guarantee a strong national authority.* [J.W., Kelowna]

Who will speak for Canadians in English Canada like myself who want a strong Federal government and also a genuine place for the aspirations of French-speaking Canadians? [I.A., Burnaby]

Lord Durham, in his famous report following the rebellions in Lower and Upper Canada in 1837, spoke of "two nations warring within the bosom of one state." What should strike the reader who examines the above statements is just how divided British Columbia opinion seems to be between the opponents and proponents of a strong federal government. In some ways, the division on this question runs even deeper than the one on Quebec, and it will surely come home to haunt BC in the event of a future "yes" vote on Quebec separation. There is a strong Canadian pole to British Columbia public opinion that may well, when push comes to shove, outweigh any inclination to further strengthen provincial power at the expense of federal power. On this issue, significant sections of BC public opinion may not see eye to eye with their elected provincial politicians. And they most certainly do not see eye to eye with majority francophone opinion in Quebec, which often sees the federal government either as an unwelcome intruder into Quebec areas of jurisdiction or as an alien entity altogether.

British Columbia as a Distinct Region

What, then, of the vision of BC regionalism that emerges from these documents? Not surprisingly, there is a significant range of views, reflecting the diversity of backgrounds of those being cited:

> We in BC live in a unique province and it is 3,000 miles from here to Ottawa and it is 10,000 miles back. When you think of that, we have always been the hind of the dog out here and to appease us every once in awhile they hang a little plum out to us and say you are BC, behave yourself. They look at the West as some obscure place on the Western planet just before Japan. [Kelowna][18]

> The current status – "Mother" Quebec and "Father" Ontario – have had their day – if not dead, "Mother" and "Father" are in their dotage. The reality of Canada in 1990 is that the "children" the provinces and territories are no longer dependent on mom and dad. The "children" have matured into adults ... The question therefore is not how to go back to "mom" and "dad" but how to get along as adults in their own right. [T.T., Peachland]

> I have lived and worked in all parts of Canada, having come from BC origins. Often, I feel that this province does not have the same sense of "country" as most other parts of Canada. [B.G., Lasqueti Island]

> The people of a region determine its unique character by their moral and ethical principles, traditions, geography, etc. ... I like the idea of a big strong country, not a divided one, but in this global economy, what happens in Japan affects me most. I cannot foresee much of a difference in my life in BC if Quebec separates. [P.C., Saltspring Island]

> Let me commend you [Glen Clark] for standing up for British Columbia rights. [M.R., White Rock]

> I love British Columbia. I don't love Quebec. When I was stationed there [during the Second World War] I never felt so foreign or disliked by many of the French speaking population ... Am I biased? You bet your life I am. But, just ask any Anglo who has recently moved here from La belle province; They will echo my words. [M.H., Surrey]

The BRITISH HERITAGE offered the diversity, tolerance and compassion and equality of opportunity which other races are now taking advantage of ... In BRITISH COLUMBIA, the unique character has been drastically altered due to the influx of immigrants encouraged to come to Canada, by an immigration policy controlled by Francophones in Ottawa! We have yet to learn whether this will enhance or shatter the BRITISH COLUMBIA character ... Keep the BRITISH in BRITISH COLUMBIA! [P. and D.G., Vancouver]

The ethnic, cultural, and racial mix of Canada is and will continue to be in a state of flux. Canadian regionalism takes on different meanings at different times. [P.G., North Vancouver]

There are a number of strongly anti-regionalist statements, however, that are also worth noting:

Not one of our elected politicians is standing up for Canada. They only seem to be talking about their regional concerns ... There's a few politicians that I'd like to send east, and I'm sure Eastern Canada has a few they'd like to send west. Until these regional differences are settled through compromise, I do not see any hope for a united Canada. [B.G., Enderby]

Those in BC who oppose a constitutional solution inevitably do so on the basis of "equality"; too many accept that argument without analysing it. Does BC want its own clause to protect French language and culture? Of course not. Does BC then want their own clause to protect the English language and culture? Hardly necessary. [G.M., Qualicum Beach]

In ways that really matter BC is not distinct from the rest of English-speaking Canada, as Mr. [Rafe] Mair claims. We speak the same language, have virtually the same civil law, and have pretty much the same culture. [H.M., Burnaby]

To the degree that a sense of BC regionalism exists, it is rooted in geography and in BC's particular cultural characteristics. It also seems, however, to be rooted in resentment of Quebec and of central Canada.

BC Separatism
A few of the briefs to the Unity Panel support BC or, in some cases, western separatism:

I've had enough. BC is well able to stand alone when [Quebec leaves]. And happen it will. [M.S., Vancouver]

Get the separation over with, dump the hegemony of Ottawa, and let BC take its proper place in the world. [P.W., Victoria]

I believe North America should be re-divided on geographical lines. I would like to see a separate country comprised of everything west of the Rockies, from Alaska to California. We have a lot more in common with Oregon and California than we do with Quebec and Newfoundland. Imagine being able to discuss salmon fishing with the Alaskans as fellow-countrymen rather than the present situation! [G.J., Port Coquitlam]

It is now more evident than ever before that the four western provinces and two western territories must now leave Canada if they do not wish to lose the last vestiges of economic, political, and social structure that have not been stripped from us to date ... In the past Canada has undergone many changes like bilingualism, federal transfers, awarding them big federal contracts etc., and yet Quebec is never satisfied ... It is now evident that Quebec intends to obtain total and independent control of its own affairs and yet will remain in Canada and retain its stranglehold on the affairs of the rest of Canada by controlling Canada's economy, government, constitution, and destiny. Since the four western provinces and the two territories economies are resource based, and have common problems, we will all be affected in one way or another. The question now remains [for the western premiers] – WHAT ARE YOU GOING TO DO FOR WESTERN CANADA? [R.S., Victoria]

Quite clearly, Quebec separatism has given rise to a BC variant, whose supporters are variously motivated by resentment of the Quebec variety or by a desire to emulate it. So far, however, if one judges from the other briefs to the Unity Panel, there seems to be significantly more opposition to than support for the idea of BC separatism:

Gordon Wilson suggests it might be a good idea if BC separates. What a novel approach to Canadian unity! Clearly Mr. Wilson does not have an open mind on the subject (let alone a particular desire to keep Canada united) and he should not be permitted to influence the Panel's process or findings to his own end. Please let the people speak and have their findings reflect accurately what they say. [G.M., Qualicum Beach]

I find the statements and musings of some provincial BC politicians, such as Pat Carney, Gordon Wilson and Glen Clark, among others, that BC may/should consider leaving Canada as downright treasonous and beyond stupidity. [R.N., "A happy, but worried Canadian," Victoria]

Why does the government of BC continually seek out confrontation with the federal government and other provinces? Why did BC invite a man who preaches sedition and treason [Gordon Wilson] to officially attend [the Unity Panel]? [W.S., Victoria]

This 82-year-old westerner (67 years in BC) is amazed that BC's most influential talk-show host, Rafe Mair, pours gasoline on the smouldering sparks of BC separatism ... According to Mr. [Gordon] Gibson and Mr. Mair there is a position to be filled: leader of a separatist movement in BC. So much for the Macdonald-Cartier vision of a nation stretching from sea to sea. Several generations and millions of Canadians who made the vision come true will have been betrayed if this country breaks up. [H.M., Burnaby]

British Columbians, who have had more than a fair share of comic-opera premiers in this century, are now listening to such siren songs as that of Senator Carney and believe that it is time to turn their back on Canada and face the promising "Pacific Rim." Hey, there's money to be made there ... or, at least, there has been, until very recently ... maybe we'll see secondary moves for independence, like Vancouver deciding that it would be better off going alone, as did Singapore, or Southern Alberta detaching itself and forming an alliance-axis with Texas. Good luck, Canada. [C.G., (no city)]

I am a Canadian first. Where I live is not as important as the idea of a unique country, and the importance of its being united, including within it a myriad of distinct, unique parts. [B.G., Lasqueti Island]

I recognize that there are many voices of dissent in the province of British Columbia, who believe that BC can survive without the rest of Canada. I am not one of these persons. I believe that a strong Canada is essential for all of us. It is time that we spoke for Canada first and devote our total energies to making Canada a better place ... there are many historic differences and shortcomings from the British Columbia perspective. We should not be consumed by these historic shortcomings, but instead commit our substantial resources to furthering an understanding of this country within the framework outlined by the Premiers in their recent Calgary initiatives. [P.P., Delta]

We in BC have lately been talking of separation ourselves ... In this sense, we're no different than Quebec: we're too busy looking out for our own interests to remember the values that are most important. [W.O., Vancouver]

A British Columbia Vision of Canada?

What is the vision of Canada to be gleaned from these briefs? There are some fairly interesting currents above and beyond a pervasive commitment to Canadian unity.

There is, for example, a strong emphasis on equality of rights and provinces and concomitant concern about according any special status to Quebec:

I would like to submit, if I may, that the underlying force which promotes unity is *equality*; the way to achieve a greater degree of unity in Canada is to strengthen equality. [P.H., Chilliwack]

We need to drop the prefixes used to describe Canadians. No more Indo-Canadians, French-Canadians, etc. We are all simply Canadians. It is time to focus on *equality* for *all* Canadians. [J.K., Mackenzie]

There is a good deal of concern about Aboriginal land claims and treaties, anticipating the divisive debate that was to accompany the tabling and passage of the Nisga'a Agreement in the BC legislature:

Aboriginal self-rule must be restricted to those powers granted to entities such as town or municipalities involving the immediate community needs but should not be granted powers normally reserved for senior governments. [M.K., Cloverdale]

There is the suggestion that language policy should best be left to the provinces:

My strong recommendation is that you repeal the Official Languages Act. This act has created more division in this country than the acceptance it was intended to generate. Let language policy be governed by the needs of individual provinces rather than by a misguided political ideology of a different era. [J.S., Victoria]

There are evocations of globalization and its effects on province and country alike:

Since Canada was formed, originally, as an economic union which is now no longer effective in the global economy that has subordinated all nation states, the question of keeping Quebec in the federation is little more than nostalgia if not irrelevant altogether. [R.O., Prince George]

I believe that the American initiative on the Multilateral Agreement on Investment, through the OECD and the APEC conferences along with the World Bank and other World Trade initiatives are geared toward securing lands, resources, and labour to serve the multinational corporate elites and usurp the national powers of sovereign states, countries and provinces ... Quebecers are nationalistic for the core social programs that define Canada as a model postwar democracy. They are modeling appropriate behaviour for the rest of Canada's sleepy little provincial territories. [P.L., Fraser Valley]

We need to appreciate that our grandchildren will need to be world citizens, not just citizens of Canada and British Columbia. We need to recognize that the future of Canada is highly dependent upon the ability of future generations to sustain the planet on which we live. We need to be clear that, if we allow the gaps between advantaged and disadvantaged to widen, there may well not be a Canada. It is in this context of Canada as a member of the world community, not only as an island onto itself, that some of the unity and constitutional debate should be carried on. [P.G., North Vancouver]

There are evocations of the need to balance rights with obligations in Canadian society:

No one can guess what will be the eventual outcome of a country minus Quebec, vast areas of land given to dozens of aboriginal bodies, & rights given to them that the rest of us don't have. How many more interest groups are there who can stake out a claim on some basis of special treatment in some aspect of life ... Everyone demands rights. No one acknowledges an obligation to community. [J.C., Vancouver]

There is concern on the part of some about the excessive divisiveness that multicultural policies foster, and praise by others for cultural diversity:

We will never have any real "Canadian unity," if we don't quit entertaining the misconception of diversity and multi-culturalism. [No name, no city]

Multiculturalism policies are fragmenting the country as they are perceived as favouritism. Political correctness has stifled expression from the general population ... Credence is given to the feminist movement to the point families are almost second fiddle to gay and lesbian relationships. Governments seem to ignore the value systems of rural people which tend to be more traditional than urban counterparts. [J.D., Port Hardy]

There is too much emphasis in this country about multiculturalism and multi ... and not enough emphasis on just being a good old Canuck. [Terrace]

I think it's great, when you look at other countries and you hear about other countries on the news, you realize that really how diverse we are in Canada and how accepting we are.[19] [Surrey]

To me, Canada is respected and recognized everywhere because it is seen as a place of opportunity, fairness, and tolerance ... This is why so many from around the world can feel welcome here and often, that is all a person will ask. [W.O., Vancouver]

There is support for a fairly hard line towards Quebec if it separates:

The Premiers of English Canada would make it abundantly clear that any *unilateral* separation from Canada by Quebec will mean a *complete* separation. Canada would defend the right of the Native population of Quebec, and other groups, to remain in Canada if they chose to do so. Quebec would be required to assume its share of the national debt. The citizens of Quebec would lose any claim to Canadian citizenship. Quebec would receive no assistance or sponsorship from Canada in its efforts to join international organizations. [A.N., Sechelt]

I say we send a clear message to Quebec. "YOU ARE WELCOME AS AN EQUAL PARTNER. BUT SHOULD YOU CHOOSE TO DIVORCE CANADA, LET'S MAKE A CLEAN AND FINAL CUT." [K.B., Abbotsford]

It is absolutely essential that the conditions of separation be absolutely clear as part of any [Quebec] referendum. Among the conditions I consider essential are: (1) A clear and ample corridor for access to the Maritimes from Ontario – perhaps a whole portion of the Eastern Townships. (2) Retention of the St. Lawrence and Seaway to Canada. (3) No Canadian parliamentary representatives for Quebec. (4) Distinct Passport, Currency. (5) Assumption of fair share of debt. [D.W., Vancouver]

There is a significant degree of emphasis on citizen democracy and institutions like constituent assemblies in mapping the future:

The present Constitution requires to be revised, a task in which Canadians at large must be involved. The Constitution being part of the evolutionary process of Common Law, belongs to the people and not the politicians. [D.A., (no city)]

At every level of government, the will of the people should be the supreme law. A "Constituent Assembly" of citizens not involved in Government or the civil service could be asked to draw up a new constitution to be ratified by the people. [P.C., Nanaimo]

Get the ordinary people of the country involved, not just those with academic excellence ... Canadians, given the chance want to participate. They do not want to be excluded by those who think they know best. The people of Canada had very little, if any, input, into our present Constitution. The world is changing rapidly, the people need to be informed and consulted. [B.E., Vernon]

If the Sovereignty of Canada were to be brought home and vested in the Citizens of Canada, the residents of Quebec would become Sovereign Citizens simultaneously with our Aboriginal People and all the rest of us ... I am sure that there are many beside myself who believe that the cement of Unity for Canada is not to be found in the power relationships between provincial and federal Governments, but is to be found in a new political and social contract between a Sovereign Citizenry and their elected governments ... I honestly believe that the First Ministers of Canada should sit this one out; what we Citizens should do is convene a Constitutional Convention to write a new Constitution for Canada based on a Sovereign Citizenry and a parliamentary democracy. [J.K., Citizen, Vancouver]

The constitution of a country ought to serve as the focal point for the collective self-image of the citizenry, and as a primary source of inspiration for their vision of the future and their aspirations for generations to come. The principles embodied in a nation's constitution, as well as its phraseology, should serve to lift a people's spirits and to challenge their sense of common purpose ... I urge members of the BC Unity Panel to raise their sights and put aside consideration of such mundane and second order issues as whether one level or another of government should have the responsibility to deliver one or another social program. I encourage you instead to focus on the crisis of legitimacy which faces our political institutions ... Fundamental to this task must be the production of substantial reforms to both our electoral and parliamentary systems. Returning power to individual parliamentarians and legislators, encouraging citizen participation in their own government, and educating Canadians ... so that they might be thoughtful and active citizens, are subjects of true importance. [D.M., West Vancouver]

There are calls for British Columbia to take the initiative in developing a new vision of Canada:

The concept of Canada as a partnership between two groups, French and English, or Quebec and the rest of Canada, was valid at the time of Confederation, when the West was insignificant and native peoples were ignored, but it is not suitable for the future. BC, as the major province which is neither Quebec nor Ontario, should take the lead in developing a new concept. [R.B., Fort Langley]

We maintain that the government of British Columbia is in a unique position to prepare a list of legitimate concerns in relation to the Canadian unity debate. We propose federal responsibility for foreign affairs, defense, trade, national standards, etc. We propose shared federal and provincial responsibilities for immigration, aboriginal affairs, appointments to the bank of Canada, Supreme Court etc. We propose provincial responsibility for levying personal and corporate taxes, language, fisheries, unemployment insurance, health, education, etc. We propose representation in both the Senate and the House of Commons be in accordance with the population of the province ... We propose that the government of British Columbia assume the leadership role in promoting a renewed and united Canada. [E. and A.S., Richmond]

If the next Quebec referendum is successful for the Parti Quebecois and they wish to begin a negotiation of separation, I would suggest an offering of a new format for our country be made. It would be called the United Nations of Canada and would include the Nation of Quebec (French Canada), the Nation of English Canada, and the Aboriginal Nations. [V.H., Kelowna]

Do these briefs provide us with what one might be tempted to call a British Columbia public philosophy? Probably not. The views that have been outlined are too varied, too opposed to one another, to add up to a coherent BC vision of the public good. The material that has been presented in this section, however, contains sometimes angry, sometimes poignant, and sometimes extremely thoughtful reflections on the state of the country as seen from the West Coast. That is why – at the risk of exhausting the reader's patience – I have presented such an extensive sampling of the views of a reasonably representative cross section of ordinary British Columbians. Whatever the politicians or the opinion-makers may have to say, it is crucial to have as accurate a reading as possible of the views from below – from the trenches, so to speak, of our national unity debate. For this reason, the briefs cited here – whether animated by the spirit of "unhyphenated Canadianism" or by an openness to the ideas of national and cultural diversity within the Canadian federation; by BC regionalism or by the affirmation of the primacy of Canadian national identity; by a nostalgia for the "British" past or by the evocation of a global future – merit careful reading by anyone interested in exploring the deeper sentiments of British Columbians regarding the challenges before us.

Conclusion

What overall conclusions can be drawn from the public opinion survey, the public hearings of the BC Unity Panel, and the written briefs submitted to the Unity Panel that have been the subject of this chapter? In other words, where does the *demos* in an ostensibly democratic British Columbia stand on the questions that this study has been examining?

1 Many ordinary British Columbians have a sense of BC's regional distinctiveness, but this seldom leads to support for BC separatism. On the contrary, for most British Columbians a sense of BC regional identity seems to be fully compatible with a sense of Canadian national identity. In this respect, the views of ordinary British Columbians are not unlike those of BC's opinion-makers and politicians.

2 Most British Columbians share a strong commitment to the concept of a united Canada and to such values as unity, diversity, equality, and national pride. In this respect, the values of ordinary British Columbians differ little from those of most other Canadians living outside Quebec.

3 A majority of British Columbians may well be prepared to recognize Quebec's unique character along the lines contained within the Calgary Declaration. A significant minority, however, has strong misgivings about where going down such a road may take Canada. And, in light of the Quebec referendum result of October 1995, there seems to be a gnawing sense that British Columbians, like other Canadians, need to begin preparing for the possibility of a country without Quebec.

4 There is sharp disagreement among British Columbians about the respective roles of the federal and provincial governments. Some would oppose any weakening of federal powers, others support flexibility in the distribution of powers between the two levels of government, and still others would support greater devolution of power to the provinces. The diversity of views of ordinary British Columbians on this subject matches that of British Columbia opinion-makers. British Columbia's politicians have often acted as though there were overwhelming grassroots support for greater provincial power, but this does not seem to be the case.

5 There are calls for greater citizen participation in political decision making and for an enhanced role for BC in developing alternative visions of Canada. To date, however, the latter desire does not seem to be reflected in the actions of BC politicians or opinion-makers. BC politicians, as I suggested in the conclusion to Chapter 2, have taken something of a backseat position when it comes to constitutional matters. The BC public may actually expect more from its leaders in articulating a vision of country than the leaders have been delivering until now.

5
A Region-Province?

British Columbia is not simply a replica of other places; it is
unique and special. And it is that uniqueness that British
Columbia's historians should be concerned to define ... We
need to work through the welter of mere information and
make more sense of what it all means for defining this very
particular province.

– Robin Fisher

The time has come to pull together some of the threads of this study.
I think Robin Fisher put his finger on something very important in
the above passage.[1] It is the need for BC historians – and, by exten-
sion, BC political scientists, sociologists, economists, literary scholars,
geographers, and others – to think in more global terms about the
society in which they live. It is the need, once they have engaged in
more empirical types of inquiry, such as Chapters 2 to 4 of this study,
to take the next step and force themselves to confront the larger questions that their data pose.

How significant is the sense of a BC regional identity? What impact has globalization had on contemporary definitions of British
Columbia? Is there a commonalty of views among politicians, opinion-
makers, and ordinary British Columbians about the province in which
they live, or are fragmentation and discord the rule? Is there a BC vision
of Canada, or is any attempt to discern one as futile as the medieval
search for the Holy Grail? Can one compare BC regionalism to Quebec nationalism, and what larger conclusions might one draw about
the different kinds of units that constitute the Canadian federation?

Regions come in different shapes and sizes, as Michael Keating
observes in his study of regionalism in Western Europe:

Where the elements of geography, economic cohesion, cultural identity,
administrative apparatus, popular identity, and territorial mobilization
coincide in space, we have a strong regionalism. In other cases, the definition of regional space is contested or regionalism is expressed in different forms across the economic, cultural and political dimensions.[2]

One can have a strong sense of regionalism in certain places, such as Flanders, Scotland, Catalonia, Andalucia, and northern Italy, and a weaker one in others, such as Wallonia, England, various parts of Germany, and the central part of Spain.[3] Where linguistic or cultural differences are crucial variables, regionalism can overlap with a distinct sense of national identity; Quebec comes to mind in the Canadian case. But regional consciousness can also be a function of geographical location, of a specific economic orientation (for example, resource exploitation), of population inflow, or of new patterns of integration into the larger global economy. These and related factors have been at work in shaping BC regionalism in the contemporary period.

Overall, there is a reasonably strong sense in British Columbia of constituting a region apart. Politicians, opinion-makers, and ordinary citizens cited in earlier chapters refer to BC's distinctiveness, to its hedonism, to its marginality, to its rebelliousness, to its utopianism, to its Western location, and so on. To this has been added in recent times an emphasis on BC's Pacific Rim orientation; its increasingly multicultural population; the fairly strong environmental consciousness of its inhabitants; and for some, though not for others, the search for a new relationship with its constituent Aboriginal population.

Globalization poses new challenges and may be preparing the ground for a new kind of regionalism, attuned to international markets. Such a regionalism is likely to be proactive rather than defensive in articulating its economic interests, and quite open to increasing connections with the outside world. For certain commentators, it also heralds the eclipse of the traditional nation-state. Kenichi Ohmae has argued:

> The modern nation state – that artifact of the 18th and 19th centuries – has begun to crumble ... Buffeted by sudden changes in industry dynamics, available information, consumer preferences and flows of capital, these political aggregations no longer make compelling sense as discrete, meaningful units on an up-to-date map of economic activity.[4]

Colin Williams, a student of European regionalism, writes:

> Regions have created an alternative agenda with a renewed sense of purpose and economic direction which has much to do with promoting the regional identity as the basic building block of European history. A "Europe of the Regions" vision ... is ... one of the most powerful visions of a refashioned Europe.[5]

And Tom Courchene, focusing on the Ontario scene, observes:

> Heartland Ontario, once so linked politically and economically with
> Ottawa that it was never even considered a "region," is now emerging as
> North America's premier *economic region state* (or *economic nation state* or
> simply *region state*, terms that we shall employ interchangeably).[6]

Are they right to see region-states sooner or later displacing the nation-
state as the prime political unit at the global level?

I am far from convinced by such arguments. There is a tendency
on the part of writers like Ohmae to read observable economic trends
such as regional clustering as harbingers of a wholesale remaking of
our geopolitical landscapes. Yet one has the right to ask whether Baden-
Würtemberg and the upper Rhine, or the growth triangle anchored
in Singapore, or the Silicon Valley/Bay Area, to cite but three examples he gives in his book,[7] are about to give the nation-state a run for
its money. Ohmae is guilty of a one-factor interpretation of contemporary global tendencies. In particular, he reduces the political and
the state to little more than handmaidens of global markets, arguing
that region-states can perform the function of "port of entry" to the
global economy better than the largely outdated nation-state can.[8]

Maybe they can in certain instances. Undoubtedly, old notions of
state sovereignty and impermeable boundaries associated with an earlier model of European-derived statehood have lost credence in an era
of global trade, capital flows, and new information technologies. But
in movements now afoot to rethink global politics, at either the continental or planetary level, there is little evidence that nation-states
do not remain the prime actors. This is as true within the European
Union (EU) as it is within the North American Free Trade Agreement
(NAFTA) or Asia-Pacific Economic Cooperation (APEC) or Mercosur; it
is as true for the North Atlantic Treaty Organization (NATO) as it is
for the United Nations. If anything, the intensity with which various
nationalist movements around the world continue to seek the coveted
status of nation-state (rather than region or minority nationality or,
worst of all, stateless nation) belies Ohmae's jejune assumptions.
(Interestingly, Williams, whom I cited earlier on European regionalism, recognizes that a regionalized vision of Europe "is still a long
way removed from economic reality."[9])

Nor is Tom Courchene any more convincing in his arguments. He
uses terms all too loosely, as the quotation above underlines. Ontario

seems to be simultaneously *economic region state, economic nation state,* or simply *region state*. Yet these words are not simply interchangeable. *Nation* carries a far deeper emotional charge than *region*. It speaks, to invoke the language of the great nineteenth-century French theorist of nationalism, Ernest Renan, to "a grand solidarity constituted by the sentiment of sacrifices which one has made and those that one is disposed to make again. [The nation] supposes a past, it renews itself especially in the present by a tangible deed: the approval, the desire, clearly expressed, to continue the communal life."[10] To turn the term *nation* into nothing more than an adjunct of specific economic activities is to engage in a form of vulgar economic determinism that makes Marxism-Leninism look almost sophisticated. Nor is it clear that the term *state,* rooted as it is in concepts such as sovereignty, legitimacy, citizenship, and the like,[11] is the right term to apply to regional actors like Canadian provinces, for these operate within a larger federal system with a central state structure that gives the constituent units much of their legitimacy.

In my opinion, Courchene is trying by some kind of economic fiat to turn Ontario into a quasi–nation-state actor, making light in the process of the powerful political, cultural, geographic, and social ties that make Ontario a constituent part of a "state" called Canada. I have yet to see evidence that any significant section of Ontario opinion – across its polarized party lines – conceives of Ontario as a region-state in the way that Courchene suggests. On the contrary, a sense of Canadian identity prevails, as well it should.

National identities have political consequences that in turn spill over into the economic arena. Helliwell and McCallum have made a fairly convincing argument for this in the case of Canada:

> In a borderless world, trade between Quebec and California should be about 10 times the value of trade between Quebec and British Columbia ... In reality, in 1988-89 the value of Quebec–British Columbia trade was 2.6 times greater than the value of Quebec-California trade.
>
> British Columbia is the same distance from Texas as from Ontario ... in a borderless world, British Columbia should trade much more with Texas than with Ontario. In reality, in 1988-89 British Columbia–Texas trade was less than one-tenth the value of British Columbia–Ontario trade.[12]

Political ties, legal arrangements, community of sentiments, and the like continue to dictate patterns of interaction that give one's own fellow citizens privileges over others. This remains true even in a world of common markets and free trade arrangements. So partly on empirical grounds, partly because of the ideological baggage that accompanies his use of the construct, I reject the term *region state* that Courchene seeks to introduce.

This does not mean that I reject the importance of region or regionalism as forms of identity. Nor does it mean that we ought not to try to come up with a term that better addresses regional loyalties in places like Ontario or British Columbia. We need to do so, however, in a way that recognizes the existence of nested territorial identities in a federal state such as Canada. Such identities are better seen as overlapping than as rival contenders for a single coveted prize.

Let me refer to the logo that the British Columbia government deployed in its media publications and advertising for the now controversial 1997 APEC summit in Vancouver. In trying to transmit the

BRITISH COLUMBIA
Canada's Pacific Gateway

message of "British Columbia Gateway to the Pacific Century," the BC government used a stylized gateway symbol, containing five blocks symbolizing BC's mountains, waters, forests, fish, and (more debatable, given the annual rainfall levels!) sunshine. It also saw fit, however, to include as a sixth block the Canadian maple leaf, making it the foundation stone underpinning the other five elements.

I see in this an eloquent testament to the relationship between regional and national identities. A region is a constituent component of a larger state structure, even though it may have important physical and cultural characteristics of its own. One is not forced to choose between being a British Columbian and being a Canadian, although that does not mean that British Columbians are the same as Manitobans, Ontarians, or Prince Edward Islanders. British Columbians see themselves as residing in a specific geographical space, namely, Canada's Pacific coast, in a landscape that combines forests, mountains, and sea. But they are no less citizens of Canada for all that, as the maple leaf on the BC logo for APEC attests.

To take this argument one step further, let us imagine an international event similar to APEC hosted by the Canadian government but being held in Quebec. Would the Quebec government, especially a Parti Québécois government, even consider the possibility of including a maple leaf, however tiny, in a logo that it used in its own media publications and advertising for the event? Of course not. To do so would mean undercutting the central claim of the sovereigntist movement, namely, that Quebec is a nation in its own right, and not a mere Canadian province or region like the others. Where the PQ is concerned, there is a zero-sum game between the recognition of Quebec's distinctiveness as a nationality and acknowledgment of Quebec's shared citizenship with other members of the Canadian federation. Although federalist-minded Quebecers would not see things in the same stark way, they too would probably see Quebec as a nation, and not simply a region of Canada. In other words, *region* and *nation* have very different places in the collective mentalities of British Columbians as opposed to Quebecers. I will come back to this shortly.

I am struck by how often BC politicians, opinion-makers, or those who submitted briefs to the 1997 BC Unity Panel have emphasized their Canadian identity. This was true for premiers like W.A.C. Bennett, as quoted in Chapter 2: "The premier is a Canadian, first, last, and all the time"; for labour leaders like Jim Kinnaird, as quoted in Chapter 3: "Working people in Western Canada are proud to be Canadians"; or for ordinary British Columbians like W.P. of West Vancouver, who was quoted in Chapter 4: "My nationality is CANADIAN. It is my BIRTHRIGHT."

If, as Renan argued, the existence of a nation is indeed "an everyday plebiscite ... a perpetual affirmation of life,"[13] British Columbians are overwhelmingly Canadian in their loyalties, just as once upon a time their predecessors were intensely British in matters imperial. Or, to put it another way, BC's inhabitants are Canadians by citizenship and national sentiment, although they may well also choose to identify themselves as British Columbians when it comes to provincial or regional identity. The notion of becoming British Columbian, as opposed to Canadian, citizens, which is what any full-fledged BC separatist movement would entail, strikes most British Columbians, whether born in the province or somewhere else, as patently absurd. It is one thing for the occasional politician or opinion-maker to threaten, in a moment of pique, that BC will take its marbles and go home, metaphorically speaking. It is quite another to think that the language of regional frustration, which in the case of BC speaks more to the pocketbook than to the heart, will trump the language of shared Canadian citizenship to the point that it sparks a viable BC separatist movement.

Blood is thicker than water, although it may be unfashionable to put it in such terms in our supposedly postmodern age, where civic, not ethnic, forms of national identity prevail and loyalties are often seen to be purely ephemeral in character. The fact remains that many British Columbians have roots and family connections in other parts of Canada; that second-, third-, or fourth-generation British Columbians have been socialized to think of themselves as inhabitants of a larger country called Canada, of which BC is a constituent part; and that new Canadians living in BC have chosen to come to a country called Canada, not British Columbia.

The desire for recognition of British Columbia as a distinct region of Canada, however, has potentially much greater appeal than any form of BC separatism. There was fairly widespread support back in 1995 – and this beyond obvious political circles – for BC acquiring a regional veto in its own right in matters constitutional, instead of simply being lumped in with the three other western provinces. There have been periodic calls for better BC representation in federal bodies such as the Bank of Canada and other federal agencies. As the poll conducted for the BC Unity Panel (see Chapter 4) showed, a good 69 percent of British Columbians felt that the province had less than its fair share of influence on national decisions; 90 percent felt that BC was underrepresented in the federal House of Commons.

What about the recurring proposal from BC governments like those of W.A.C. Bennett or Bill Bennett to remake the Senate on a five-region basis – in other words, with BC having a bloc of 24 senators alongside Atlantic Canada, Quebec, Ontario, and the three Prairie provinces? In truth, there is little evidence that this has ever caught the BC public's imagination. To the degree that the Senate has been an issue at all over the past decade, it has been cast in terms of the

Reform Party's demand for a "triple-E" Senate. Interestingly, BC would stand to gain less under such an arrangement (one senator in ten) than it would under the five-region proposal (one senator in five). This does not seem to have made the slightest difference in terms of popular support for the Reform Party. But then Senate reform, where most British Columbians are concerned, has been something of a side issue in terms of the larger region-nation debate.

Underlying the whole question of BC's recognition as a region is a sense that BC deserves a larger place in the Canadian sun. A number of factors militate in favour of the province assuming a larger role in Canadian affairs than has been its wont: (1) a burgeoning population and significant inflow of immigrants, both from within Canada and from abroad; (2) a dynamic service sector with new knowledge-based industries; (3) a future-oriented set of values in line with the information age that we have now entered; (4) location on the Pacific Ocean, one of the dynamic poles of the twenty-first-century global economy. As it is presently constituted, however, Canada's federal system is dominated by the priorities of central Canada and by a historical orientation towards Europe and the Atlantic world. And one province, Quebec, has been dominating federal politics (for example, the office of the prime minister) and the political agenda at large (for example, Canada's long-running constitutional debate) for so long that it is seen to have crowded out the no less legitimate claims of growing provinces such as British Columbia.

This helps explains the fervent opposition by many British Columbians to what have been seen as attempts by Quebec to secure special privileges, special status, distinct society status, or recognition of its unique character at the expense of the rest of Canada. People in BC were a good deal more hostile to both Meech and Charlottetown than those in almost any other province. In the aftermath of the near-victory by the "yes" side in the 1995 Quebec referendum, there was a good deal of suppressed rage in the air over the fact that British Columbians, like other Canadians outside Quebec, had been forced to watch impotently from the sidelines while the fate of their country hung in the balance. There is an angry tone to many presentations dealing with Quebec that were made to the BC Unity Panel (Chapter 4).

BC public opinion strongly favours the notion of equality of provinces, even while rejecting any simple dichotomy between a so-called English Canada and Quebec. It bristles at Quebec demands for greater recognition, all the more because Quebec is seen as having been a net beneficiary of federal largesse, patronage, and transfer payments while BC has generally not been. (That British Columbia has been a "have," not a "have-not," province makes little difference in this regard.) If I can invoke a term to encompass the underlying feeling I am trying to describe, I would call it the *politics of resentment.*

Resentment (or *ressentiment,* to use the French term more common to the social sciences) can be a powerful factor in fuelling social movements. A sense of hurt, of betrayal, of unfair treatment has often played a role in nationalist movements reacting to the vexations of powerful forces in the outside world. As Liah Greenfeld, one of the more lucid analysts of modern nationalism, puts it:

> *Ressentiment* refers to a psychological state resulting from suppressed feelings of envy and hatred (existential envy) and the impossibility of satisfying these feelings. The sociological basis for ressentiment is twofold. The first condition is ... the belief on the part of the subject in fundamental equality ... The second condition is actual inequality of such dimensions that it rules out practical achievement of the theoretically existing equality.[14]

I think some of the factors that Greenfeld cites can help explain mainstream BC reactions to Quebec nationalism. There is an element of existential envy at work, a sense that francophone Quebecers have somehow got their collective act together when Canadians living outside Quebec have not. There is a sense that francophone Quebecers, with a perfectly good conscience, have been trying to pull the wool over the collective eyes of their fellow Canadians, and that they have been getting away with it time after time. There is an element of raw antagonism on the part of many British Columbians to the project of a Quebec nationhood that is seen to threaten the very fabric of the Canadian state. There is a feeling that British Columbia, in its own way, is no less distinct a part of Canada than is Quebec, but that the pan-Canadian debate has veered off in a direction that denies their fundamental comparability. And there is a fear that Canadians are living in a version of George Orwell's *Animal Farm,* where some animals, put quite simply, are or want to be treated as more equal than others.

The politics of resentment is in a sense the flip side of what Charles Taylor has called the politics of recognition.[15] Recognition, he has argued, is what minority or historically oppressed nationalities (for example, Québécois, Aboriginal peoples) may be seeking to achieve in the contemporary world. In other words, they seek recognition of their own distinctive national identities by the majority population with whom they share a state. Furthermore, they want their fellow citizens to accept some of the community-inspired policy tools, such as language legislation like Bill 101 in Quebec, that are required to secure the minority nationality's survival. (The same logic would apply to Aboriginal land claims settlements.)

There is something of a dialogue of the deaf, I would argue, between those who demand recognition and their would-be interlocutors. For the advocates of minority nationality recognition, those who refuse or resent their claims are simply holding on to their own privileged positions as part of the dominant majority; they are incapable of understanding the existential plight that threatens the core identities of peoples with minority languages and cultures. For their interlocutors, the advocates of minority nationality recognition want to have it all their own way – recognition of their own specific needs but no countervailing willingness to recognize the legitimate needs of the other units or of the majority population with whom they share a federal state.

There is no easy way to resolve this imbroglio, which helps explain why, after several intensive rounds of constitutional debate, Canadians seem to be no further along the road to constitutional closure than before.[16] In the end, some form of mutual recognition between majority and minority nationalities, based on combining common citizenship with the acknowledgment of the multiple national identities that make up the federation, may well be the only way for a state like Canada to survive. We in Canada could use something of the subtlety that the British bring to their debate – with Scotland and Wales symbolically acknowledged as nations within the United Kingdom alongside the English. The Spanish are even more adroit in trying to reconcile the principle of a shared Spanish nationhood with the reality of minority nationalities and regional sentiments. Article 2 of their 1978 constitution reads: "The foundation of the Constitution rests on the indissoluble unity of the Spanish nation, the common and indivisible homeland of all Spaniards. The Constitution recognizes and guarantees the right of its nationalities and regions to autonomy and to solidarity with one another."[17] Spain's Statute of Autonomy, promulgated in 1981, recognizes the existence of regions that for all practical purposes are nationalities (such as Catalonia, the Basque

Country, Galicia) alongside regions that are not (such as Valencia, Andalucia, Extremadura, Asturias).

Perhaps we need a new symbolic framework for Canada as a whole. Let me advance a modest proposal towards this end. I would argue that we have provinces: Newfoundland, Nova Scotia, PEI, New Brunswick, Manitoba, Saskatchewan. We have region-provinces: Ontario, BC, and probably Alberta. And we have one nation-province, Quebec, although Newfoundlanders, in their more sentimental moments, might fancy themselves fitting this bill as well.

I am not suggesting that we constitutionalize any such arrangement in the near future; Canadians have become immunized against the "C" word in the aftermath of Meech and Charlottetown, and there is little to be gained by yet another round of rancorous constitutional debate at this time. Nor am I even certain that we need to change anything in the formal institutional structure of Canadian federalism to begin the process of rethinking its underlying *symbolic* makeup. It will suffice if for certain purposes we differentiate among the ten provinces in this manner; political restructuring may eventually follow suit.

Sociologically speaking, a three-tiered framework comes closer to describing the Canadian situation than specious calls for recognizing the formal equality of all provinces on the one hand or some grudging acknowledgment of Quebec's unique character – "nudge, nudge, wink, wink!" – on the other. Doesn't our federal system, de facto if not *de jure*, already contain three different types of actors within it? There are provinces with small populations (1 million or less), relatively dependent economies (for example, a reliance on federal transfer payments to balance their books), and fairly circumscribed geopolitical horizons. There are region-provinces with more significant population bases (3, 4, or 11 million, as the case may be); ample economic resources that make them "have" rather than "have-not" provinces; and expansive geopolitical horizons – Alberta with the American, no less than Canadian, market for its oil and gas; BC with the Pacific Northwest and Pacific Rim at its doorstep; Ontario with its auto industry and links to the Midwestern states with which it shares the Great Lakes. Finally, there is a nation-province with some 7 million people, Quebec: not as rich, relatively speaking, as the three region-provinces, but with a clearer sociological sense of constituting a nation within Canada, much like Scotland within the United Kingdom or Catalonia within Spain.

Is acknowledging Quebec's desire to be seen as a nation entirely at odds with acknowledging BC's desire to be seen as a distinct region of

Canada? I am struck by the number of references that BC politicians, opinion-makers, and ordinary citizens have made to the frequent similarity between the positions of British Columbia and Quebec when it comes to federal-provincial matters. As Rafe Mair put it: "In many ways, Quebec has been a counter-balance to Ontario in Canada's body politic. When in government, I was astonished by the number of times Quebec and British Columbia were aligned against Ontario (though, admittedly, usually not for precisely the same reasons)."[18]

This is more than a coincidence. It speaks to the desire, for certain purposes, of many in both societies to control various things at the provincial level, for regional reasons on the one hand and national reasons on the other. More importantly, it speaks to parallel feelings of constituting a society with characteristics of its own.

Is there a possible trade-off between acknowledging Quebec's status as a nation-province and BC's being seen as a region-province? Can mutual recognition replace a one-sided politics of recognition of minority nationalities on the one hand and an equally one-sided politics of resentment on the other? At first blush, the answer appears to be "no," especially if the idea of nation is equated with that of state, as it seems to be for so many on the sovereigntist side of the debate in Quebec. And there are many in British Columbia who, in reflex fashion, would equate *nation* with *state* and reject the use of the term *nation* for anything other than Canada as a whole.

Yet the usage of terms can vary considerably across language lines and communities. The use of the term *nation* has a long and venerable tradition in French Canadian political discourse, going back to the nineteenth century at least.[19] Nor is there any sign of this changing any time soon. Let me give but one illustration of what I have in mind.

During the summer of 1999, the Montreal newspaper *Le Devoir* ran a twelve-part series on its op-ed page every Saturday featuring different Quebec intellectuals – e.g., Charles Taylor, Gilles Bourque, Jocelyn Letourneau, Gerard Bouchard – writing on the theme *Penser la nation québécoise – Thinking about the Quebec nation.*[20] Some were federalist-leaning, some were sovereigntist-leaning; most were interested in going beyond old nostrums about national identity, recognizing the increasingly multicultural, pluralist character of Quebec society today. The point I want to make is a straightforward one. It is hard to imagine Ontario or BC newspapers running a twelve-part series on Ontario or BC as a nation (just as it is hard to imagine the term *intellectual* being used in the same positive way in English as it is commonly used in French).

Simply put, Ontario or BC or Alberta are not nations in the sociological sense of the term. Their inhabitants may well have a sense of regional identity, some a very strong one, but they do not think of themselves, linguistically or culturally, as constituting a national community of their own. Most Quebecers do, with the real divide between federalists and sovereigntists revolving around the question of whether this sense of nationality can be better realized within a larger Canadian ensemble or outside it. There have already been two referenda on this question, with a third one still very much a possibility somewhere down the line.

To date there has been no referendum asking the people of British Columbia whether BC constitutes a distinct region of Canada, and one wonders what the point of any such exercise would be. As Michael Keating argues:

> Regions must be seen as open systems rather than self-contained societies. They are partial social systems linked functionally to other levels, rather than the global societies encompassing the totality of social relationships which are the traditional aspiration of the nation state. For this reason, regionalism is not an alternative principle of organization to the state. Regions rarely seek to displace states or take over the state functions of regulation and legitimation.[21]

Those seeking to assert their regional identity do not feel the same passion that one finds in those asserting their national identity. Most of BC's inhabitants would have little difficulty thinking of BC as a region; for certain purposes – lifestyle, political culture, social mores, trading patterns – BC stands apart from the rest of Canada, looking inward at times, southward at others, or westward across the Pacific. At the same time, in an era of globalization, NAFTA, and the like, the region represents a significant pole of identity alongside local, national, and, increasingly, transnational poles. As the European Union's Committee of the Regions argues: "At present, people can accept globalization, and be part of Europeanization, only if they feel that their national, regional and local identities are not being lost."[22]

In acknowledging the things that make BC distinct, we need to be careful to keep things in perspective. As Chapters 3 and 4 in particular have shown, many British Columbians identify with federal institutions to a significant degree. This should not surprise us, because for British Columbians, as for most other Canadians outside Quebec, the federal government represents their *national* government. Many also have a keen sense of the limitations of a purely provincial/regional pole of identity, all the more given the antics and comic opera features that have for too long characterized BC politics. There may be a significant difference in this regard between popular and elite opinion. As Roger Gibbins has argued: "Regionalism may be more salient to political elites than to the mass public, it may affect elite political behaviour more than mass political behaviour, and the regional conception of Canada championed by provincial politicians may not be completely shared by their electorates."[23]

The concept of national identity is far from obsolete as we enter the twenty-first century. Market economics and capital flows are one thing, political and cultural reference points another. The very forces of globalization that weaken national sovereignty on the one hand may, paradoxically, be strengthening a concern for cultural specificity and national rootedness on the other. Unlike Quebec sovereigntists who dream of the fleur-de-lis flying at the United Nations, British Columbians, with the occasional exception of a few politicians, ex-politicians, and talk show hosts, do not dream of BC becoming a sovereign state. Nor do they aspire to seeing BC become a largely self-governing region-state, to invoke Tom Courchene's term. What they aspire to is recognition of BC as an important actor within the Canadian federation, an actor that is both a self-defined region and a province of Canada. Where provincial/regional interests predominate, political power needs to be exercised provincially/regionally; where national coordination and direction are required, federal powers should prevail.

Most British Columbians, I would hazard to guess, would be quite comfortable seeing BC defined as a region-province of Canada. And it may just be that a three-tiered vision of Canada – six provinces, three region-provinces, and one nation-province – might constitute a useful BC contribution to the national unity debate. Such a vision might allow us to move beyond the constructs of ten equal provinces, or five regions, or two founding peoples that have dominated the political discussion until now. It might represent a symbolic way of reconciling the deep-rooted desire for national recognition in Quebec with the widespread desire in British Columbia to be seen as a region in its own right.

In concrete terms, what might my three-tiered proposal entail? De facto, under such a scheme Quebec would receive recognition as a distinct society within Canada where language, culture, and civil law are concerned. The Quebec government would be freer to exercise the sort of powers it has already acquired pursuant to legislation like Bill 101. It might also open the door to greater Quebec powers in the future in areas currently under federal jurisdiction. The quid pro quo for this, however, would almost certainly be a reduced role for Quebec's federal representatives in Ottawa in those areas from which Quebec had withdrawn.

The situation resembles that which the United Kingdom may face as the devolution of powers to Scotland and Wales progresses. To the degree that significant powers come to be vested in the Scottish and Welsh assemblies, there may be growing pressure from England to see Scottish and Welsh influence over decision making in Westminster reduced. In much the same way, an enhanced Quebec nation-province could not hope to play the same role in decision making for the rest of Canada at the federal level as could the province of Quebec.

Where the three region-provinces are concerned, they would not be seeking formal powers greater than those of the six ordinary provinces. De facto, however, where constitutional change is concerned, they already wield veto powers that the other provinces individually do not have. And they would have economic resources at their disposal and a tax base that permits them a good deal more autonomy in decision making than their poorer provincial counterparts.

It may also turn out to be the case that in any future Senate reform, region-provinces like British Columbia and Alberta, no less than Ontario, may secure stronger representation than the six smaller provinces. (I return to this theme in the concluding chapter.) They would also have strong claims to having their voices heard where important federal agencies are concerned.

I remind the reader, however, that in this chapter I have been less interested in setting out a detailed institutional model of how a three-tiered Canada might operate than in advancing the idea that a new way of thinking about Canada is required. Whether or not we adopt the terminology of *nation-province, region-province,* and *province,* the fact remains that British Columbia – like Ontario and increasingly Alberta – has legitimate claims to be thought of as constituting a region, and not only a province, of Canada.

6
What If?

Most British Columbians would like to see Canada continue as a single country stretching from sea to sea to sea. They would like to see Quebec continue as a full partner in Confederation; if their views at the time of the Calgary Declaration and the BC Unity Panel deliberations are anything to go by, British Columbians might well be prepared to recognize Quebec's unique character when it comes to language, culture, and civil law. Perhaps, in some future restructuring of the federation, they might even be prepared to acknowledge Quebec's status as a nationality or nation-province within Canada, although the quid pro quo might have to be a symbolic acknowledgment of BC's status as a region-province of Canada and an enhanced role for BC in federal affairs.

We need to be realistic and level-headed in our thinking, however. We are not facing any imminent constitutional negotiations. Instead, there is every possibility that the Parti Québécois government headed by Lucien Bouchard (or his successor) will call a third Quebec referendum, if not during its current mandate then during a subsequent mandate. The question of Quebec sovereignty would once again be front and centre in the political debate.

I thought it would be useful, therefore, in a short concluding chapter, to offer my thoughts on how British Columbia politicians, opinion-makers, and public opinion are likely to respond to such an eventuality. More pertinently, I thought it important to map out the likely BC response to a "yes" vote in a third Quebec referendum – a vote opening the door to Quebec sovereignty.

What follows, of course, is highly speculative in character. It assumes, in light of the Supreme Court of Canada judgment of August 1998, that a "yes" result would be based on a clear majority of Quebecers voting "yes" to a clear question on sovereignty.[1] This could prove to be quite a difficult test to meet in the absence of prior agreement on the referendum question between sovereigntists and federalists in Quebec, and between the Quebec and Canadian governments. What constitutes a clear question? What constitutes a clear majority? Are Bernard Landry and Stéphane Dion ever likely to see eye to eye on this? Will the federal government's recently passed Clarity Bill make this any easier?

Let us somehow assume that these hurdles have been overcome. Let us also assume that a clear majority of Quebecers – whether the figure turns out to be 52.5 percent or 57.5 percent or 62.5 percent – do in fact vote "yes" to a clear question on sovereignty. And let us further assume that there is none of the controversy about spoiled ballots that marred the 1995 Quebec referendum and that could have led to a serious questioning of the results had the "yes" side, rather than the "no" side, won by the slimmest of margins.[2]

Faute de mieux, then, Canadians in other provinces would need to reconcile themselves to the inevitable. Lucien Bouchard (or some future Parti Québécois leader) would have somehow succeeded in mobilizing Quebec public opinion yet again, turning around pre-election polls predicting a "no" victory. Jean Chrétien (or his successor) would be left with little but their hollow reassurances to the Canadian electorate that Quebecers would never leave "the best country in the world." What then?

A whole series of issues would need to be negotiated. There would be the question of Aboriginal peoples in Quebec, especially those in northern Quebec, who have made abundantly clear their desire to continue to be part of Canada whatever the outcome of a future Quebec referendum.[3] There would be the question of ongoing Canadian citizenship for anglophones, allophones, and even francophone federalists who wished to retain their Canadian affiliation. The issue of partition might arise, all the more if, as in the past, a majority of voters in the Outaouais region of Quebec, in the Greater Montreal area, and in the Eastern Townships voted "no." There would be the ticklish question of division of the federal debt – on a demographic basis, as Canadians outside Quebec would insist, or perhaps on a per capita income basis, as Quebec sovereigntists are likely to insist.[4] There would be the question of assured air, road, and rail links between Ontario and Atlantic Canada. There would be the question of international recognition of Quebec sovereignty and of Quebec's accession to international agreements such as the North American Free Trade Agreement (NAFTA). Finally, there would be the question of partnership, since more likely than not the offer of partnership to Canada would have been part of any winning sovereignty referendum.

There is little doubt that a post–Quebec referendum federal government would need to negotiate many of these points with a victorious sovereigntist government in Quebec. Indeed, the same Supreme Court judgment that laid out the "clear majority on a clear question" conditions for a future Quebec referendum vote also stated a requirement for good-faith negotiations by the parties in the event of a winning "yes" vote.[5] Who exactly would sit in the Canadian delegation is uncertain. It would certainly be awkward to have elected federal politicians from Quebec negotiating the separation of Quebec from Canada on behalf of the rest of the country. There would also be strong pressure to ensure that the nine remaining provinces were part of any negotiations that ensued. British Columbians would be in the forefront in voicing such a demand.

I suspect that the question of partitioning Quebec would probably not get off the ground, for the simple reason that secessions involving boundary changes can be a good deal nastier than secessions that do not. One need only compare the relatively "velvet" divorce that followed the breakup of Czechoslovakia with the series of wars that followed the breakup of Yugoslavia. Everything in the Canadian and Quebec political tradition, in my opinion, militates in favour of a Czechoslovak rather than a Yugoslav scenario. The question of the Aboriginal population of Quebec is a delicate one, however, that may well require some kind of shared Canada-Quebec responsibility into the future.[6] As for minority language rights, each of the successor states would have an interest in assuring equitable treatment for its official language minority. For Quebec would know full well that there were Franco-Canadians outside its borders, just as a post-Quebec Canada would know that there were Anglo-Quebecers within Quebec's. Still, I for one do not believe that official bilingualism would long survive in a post-Quebec Canada, and British Columbia's would be one of the loudest voices demanding its abrogation.

Where BC would likely prove particularly intransigent is on the idea of any partnership between Canada and a sovereign Quebec. Let me quote one more time comments made by two BC premiers at the time of the two previous Quebec referenda. Bill Bennett, speaking in Montreal in May 1980, stated:

> I would be remiss if I did not restate my firm opposition to the concept
> of "sovereignty-association." [It] offers British Columbians no spirit, no
> heart, no common purpose and no goals. The bottom line of nationhood
> is not to be found on a balance sheet ... Remove nationhood and the
> commitment to sacrifice some regional advantages goes with it ... A sov-
> ereign Quebec would become a foreign country with whom we would
> treat exclusively on a basis of self interest.[7]

For his part, Mike Harcourt, not the most pit-bullish of BC premiers,
stated in May 1994: "If somebody tried to break up this country, we
should be the worst of enemies. It's not going to be civilized. It's not
going to be over tea with our pinkies out."[8] Let me also quote again
from two prominent BC opinion-makers on opposite sides of the political spectrum. For Gordon Gibson, "sovereignty-association will not
be accepted by the other provinces! Do not go down this road, for on
that road lies disaster."[9] And for Tom Berger, "sovereignty association
is an attempt to have it both ways ... For Quebec it must be a moment
of truth, unobscured by soothing sounds from English Canada about
accommodating Quebec in some absurdist confederal state."[10]

In the spring of 1999, the Bloc Québécois published a document
outlining its proposals for partnership between a sovereign Quebec
and Canada. There are five different scenarios: (1) informal economic
integration, (2) economic union, (3) economic union with sectoral
political partnerships, (4) economic union with confederation, and
(5) economic union with confederal and federal arrangements.[11] It
leaves it up to Quebec and Canada to define the scope of any future
arrangements, on the basis of equality between the two partners and
acceptance of Quebec sovereignty.[12] There is little doubt in my mind
that the mood in British Columbia would be completely opposed to
everything encompassed in options 2 to 5. I need but remind the
reader of some of the venomous comments about Quebec recorded
in Chapter 4 to underline the angry mood likely to result from a successful "yes" vote in Quebec.

At best there might be a grudging acceptance of option 1, informal
economic arrangements, for example, through NAFTA, once contentious issues such as division of the national debt had been worked
out. Arrangements that involved formal political structures between
Canada and Quebec, however, with the likelihood of a Quebec veto
built in, would simply prove unacceptable to BC public opinion. The
ties of sentiment that currently bind British Columbia to Quebec

would be totally transformed once Quebec's inhabitants ceased to be citizens of a common Canadian state. There would be no shortage of voices in British Columbia seeking to cut ties with Quebec to less than zero, if possible.

Under the circumstances, the priority for British Columbians would not be forging partnership arrangements with a departed Quebec. Rather, it would lie in addressing the future of a post-Quebec Canada. This would mean rethinking the map of a country that excluded Quebec. It would involve some fairly serious rethinking and restructuring of the Canadian federation. Moreover, all this would likely occur in a context where there were calls for BC (or the West) to go it alone, given the weight of Ontario in a post-Quebec Canada.

Alan Cairns, my longtime colleague in the Department of Political Science at the University of British Columbia, offered some sage advice at a conference in Vancouver in March 1997. He suggested that there be a three- to five-year moratorium on intra-Canadian constitutional negotiations in the aftermath of a "yes" vote in a future Quebec referendum, to allow time for the full impact of Quebec's departure to sink in. I think he is right, although it remains to be seen whether a majority of British Columbians (and other Canadians) would concur.

One thing I can predict, if and when constitutional negotiations to restructure a post-Quebec Canada begin, is that British Columbia will spearhead the call for some kind of elected constituent assembly. After all, BC is a province that has legislation on the books providing for citizen initiatives, recall, and referenda on major constitutional changes. A fair amount of concern about citizen democracy was expressed in the briefs to the BC Unity Panel cited in Chapter 4. British Columbians would certainly demand significant input into the process by which a new Canadian constitution comes to be written. Albertans would inexorably back them in this. An elected constituent assembly would therefore figure prominently in any future constitutional debate and would need to be addressed.

What about the substance of any new Canadian constitution? British Columbia, as the second largest province in a post-Quebec Canada, would be a strong advocate of rebalancing the federation. Ontario by itself would constitute about 50 percent of the Canadian population. With representation by population as the basis for allocating seats in the House of Commons, there would be every likelihood of an Ontario with 50 percent of the seats dominating federal politics. We have seen how important a monolithic Liberal caucus from Ontario has proven to be in the operation of the Liberal government in power in

Ottawa since 1993. Would a post-Quebec Canada be facing something similar?

There are two different ways of addressing this problem: proportional representation and Senate reform. (Some would suggest a third option – splitting Ontario into two or more provinces – but I don't think this proposition is seriously on.) Proportional representation as it has been practised in West Germany or, more recently, in elections to the Scottish and Welsh assemblies, would put an end to a first-past-the-post system that allows parties with barely 40 percent of the popular vote to stack up large parliamentary majorities. Instead, proportional representation would ensure that all parties that capture at least 5 percent of the overall popular vote, or that have been able to elect candidates at the constituency level, would be represented in Parliament, in numbers roughly proportionate to their popular support. Under such an arrangement, Ontario would be no more likely to elect a caucus made up of 99 percent Liberals than Alberta would be to elect one made up only of Reformers or members of the Canadian Alliance. Rather, the different political parties would be better represented within the different provincial caucuses. We would also be more likely to see coalition governments.

Even with proportional representation, however, Ontario would still account for the lion's share of seats in a future Canadian House of Commons. Some attention would therefore need to be paid to Senate reform. If we were to retain an upper house in the future – and almost all the provinces of outer Canada would demand this – it clearly would have to be an elected and not an appointed body. How would the different provinces be represented?

The proponents of a "triple-E" Senate – elected, effective, equal – clearly had the American or Australian models in mind. In both countries, each state has equal representation in the Senate – two per state in the United States, twelve per state in Australia. Despite population differences, Vermont and California have two senators each, and Tasmania has the same number of senators as New South Wales. Is this necessarily the best model to adopt for Canada?

The Germans, who have been quite successful in operating their federal system since 1949, do not provide for equal representation for their Länder in the Federal Council, or Bundesrat. Larger Länder, such as North Rhine–Westphalia or Bavaria, have larger delegations in the Bundesrat than smaller Länder, such as Hamburg or Bremen. Why shouldn't we follow their example? Provinces with large populations, say more than 7.5 million inhabitants, could have 24 senators under such a scheme. Provinces with 2.5 to 7.5 million inhabitants could have half that number, 12 senators each. Provinces with less than 2.5 million inhabitants could have half that number again, 6 senators each. And the territories could each have a senator as well. For the foreseeable future, this would translate into an 87-seat Senate. Ontario would have 24 senators; BC and Alberta 12 senators each; Newfoundland, Nova Scotia, PEI, New Brunswick, Manitoba, and Saskatchewan 6 senators each; and the territories 1 senator each.

Ontario would account for about 27 percent of the members in such a body, the two westernmost provinces for about 13.5 percent each, and the smaller provinces for about 7 percent each. Under such an arrangement, the West would have 41 percent of the total membership in the Senate, and Atlantic Canada would have the same 27 percent share as Ontario. The western provinces together with Atlantic Canada would clearly outnumber Ontario, but Ontario along with BC and Alberta would outnumber the smaller provinces, and Ontario along with Atlantic Canada would outnumber the West. Given party allegiances among senators, however, it is by no means obvious that bloc voting along provincial lines would normally be the rule.

A further question that would need to be tackled relates to the powers the Senate would exercise. If it were to have equal powers with the House of Commons, there would be every possibility of conflicting majorities in the two chambers, and of eventual gridlock. It is normal, under the British system of parliamentary government that Canada has inherited, to vest greater powers in the House of Commons. It would therefore make more sense to give the Senate a suspensive veto in matters that are exclusively federal, but to give it an absolute veto in matters where provincial interests are more directly at stake. Votes of confidence would continue to be the prerogative of the House of Commons.

The distribution of powers between the federal and provincial governments would be the subject of extensive debate in any future constituent assembly. There would be strong pressure from provincial governments such as British Columbia's for greater provincial jurisdiction in areas such as labour market training, fisheries, and so on. There would also be insistence on equal treatment of all provinces where joint federal-provincial programs were concerned. And one could expect demands for a share of appointments to all federal agencies and bodies commensurate with BC's place in the renewed federation.

Once one goes beyond these sorts of demands, I'm not convinced there would be any easy agreement among British Columbians. As

Chapter 4 has shown, there is considerable support for strong federal powers in British Columbia – far more than regionalist spokespersons would let on. In a post-Quebec Canada, it is quite possible that nationalist sentiment would be much stronger than at present. When people fear for the very survival of their country, they are likely to rally to its defence with renewed fervour. Many in British Columbia would feel the need to strengthen, not weaken, shared national bonds with their fellow Canadians in a country without Quebec. In other words, Quebec's secession may have more of a nationalizing than a regionalizing effect on BC public opinion.

Although it may not be politically correct to say so, I believe that a post-Quebec Canada would have considerably more cohesion as a nation-state than Canada with Quebec. Linguistically and culturally, Canada would be much closer to the American, Australian, or German model of federation – a territorial or unilingual model – than before. The federal government would be the national government of all Canadians in a way that has not really been true where many in Quebec have been concerned. A post-Quebec Canada would have shed something of Canada's present multinational character, but it would have gained coherence and unity of purpose in the process. Under such circumstances, British Columbians are likely to prove just as Canadian in their sentiments as anyone else.

This is the main reason that I, for one, do not take the threat of BC separatism that seriously. (Nor does the evidence provided in Chapters 3 and 4 suggest that we ought to.) Undoubtedly there would be voices saying that BC should go its own way. There would be concerns about the Pakistanization of Canada – with Atlantic Canada physically cut off from Ontario and the West. There would be finger-pointing at Ontario. There would be talk about Cascadia – although there is no evidence that the United States is about to fragment along regional fault lines, or that Washington, Oregon, and Alaska are particularly keen to hook up with BC to form a new country. In short, BC separatism would become a threat only if the Canadian national will falters in the aftermath of Quebec's separation, and if our politicians are unable to get their act together and renew the Canadian federation in a democratic and regionally sensitive fashion. My hunch is that Canadians are not likely to let this happen.

How would British Columbians view a written Charter of Rights and Freedoms in any new Canadian constitution, and the role of the courts in interpreting it? How would they view official multiculturalism? How would they view Aboriginal issues? How would they see the role of the Canadian dollar, particularly if it were greatly weakened as a result of the Quebec secession crisis? Would there be a hot debate about retaining the monarchy? I do not want to press my luck any further when it comes to crystal-ball gazing, but these are among the issues that would need to be tackled.

The fact remains that a large majority of British Columbians, including this author, would prefer that Canada survive as a single, undiminished state. Something very important would have been lost if the Canada that was created in 1867 were to expire. And the negative example we would be providing for other multinational federations around the world would be a sobering one indeed. The fact also remains, however, that British Columbians are prepared to begin thinking about life without Quebec and have informed their provincial government that it ought to be making preparations for such an eventuality. (As mentioned in Chapter 4, 78 percent of respondents to the BC Unity Panel survey felt this way.)

BC would have a pivotal role to play in any remaking of Canada following a "yes" vote in Quebec. Unlike in 1864-67, BC and the other western provinces would be in on the ground floor. The result would be a much greater sensitivity all around to western Canada's place in the larger scheme of things. As the second most populous province in the country and as a region in its own right, British Columbia would be expected to provide no small part of the leadership and vision required for nation building in the new Canada. British Columbians could not sit this round out, narcissistically contemplating their navels.

Is British Columbia up to the challenge? Can a province that for so long has seen itself on the periphery of the federation suddenly begin to play such a different role? There is a streak in BC political culture, a petty provincialism and indifference to the world east of the Rockies, which could easily undermine any such endeavour. There is also, however, a BC tradition of rising to new challenges, of accepting one's citizenship duties and obligations within the larger Canadian scheme of things, that could serve the cause of post-Quebec Canadian unity very well. Let us hope that the latter prevails if and when British Columbians have to face the question "What if?" For if the politics of resentment provides an insufficient basis for regional self-affirmation, it provides an even weaker basis for the renewal of national identity that, with or without Quebec, confronts the Canada of the future.

Notes

Chapter 1: BC as a Distinct Region of Canada

1 Amor de Cosmos, cited in Miro Cernetig, "The Far Side of the Rockies: Politics and Identity in British Columbia," in *A Passion for Identity*, ed. David Taras and Beverley Rasporich (Toronto: Nelson, 1997), 452.

2 Employers' Council of British Columbia, *Populism, Partisanship, and Progress* (Vancouver, November 1978), 34.

3 From a letter by Macdonald to the Marquess of Lorne dated 11 July 1883, cited in Garth Stevenson, *Ex Uno Plures* (Montreal: McGill-Queen's University Press, 1993), 141. Interestingly, the British colonial secretary, Lord Kimberley, had referred to British Columbia as "the spoilt child of Confederation" two years earlier. See Margaret Ormsby, *British Columbia: A History* (Toronto: Macmillan, 1958), 283.

4 Peter Robert Hunt, "The Political Career of Sir Richard McBride" (MA thesis, University of British Columbia, 1953).

5 Duff Pattullo, cited in Robin Fisher, *Duff Pattullo of British Columbia* (Toronto: University of Toronto Press, 1991), 333.

6 W.A.C. Bennett, cited in Roger Keene and David Humphreys, eds., *Conversations with W.A.C. Bennett* (Toronto: Methuen, 1980), 96.

7 Daphne Bramham, "Premier Will Demand Provincial Control Over Fishery," *Vancouver Sun*, 25 May 1996, B3.

8 Robert Greenhow, *The History of Oregon and California and the Other Territories of the North-West Coast of North America* (1845), cited in Craig Donald Andrews, "BC: A Study of the Themes of Hardship and a Sterile Land upon Its Literature, both Descriptive and Historical, 1628-1914" (MA thesis, Washington State University, 1968), 52.

9 John McLean, *Notes of a 25 Years Service in the Hudson Bay Territory*, cited in Andrews, "BC: A Study of the Themes of Hardship," 72.

10 D.G.F. Macdonald, *British Columbia and Vancouver's Island* (London, 1862), cited in Andrews, "BC: A Study of the Themes of Hardship," 92.

11 Maria Tippett and Douglas Cole, *From Desolation to Splendour: Changing Perceptions of the British Columbia Landscape* (Toronto: Clarke, Irwin, 1977), 141.

12 R.E. Gosnell, *History of British Columbia* (Vancouver and Victoria, 1913), cited in Allan Smith, *Canada: An American Nation?* (Montreal: McGill-Queen's University Press, 1994), 200-1 ("Defining British Columbia").

13 Emily Carr, cited in Jean Barman, *The West beyond the West: A History of British Columbia,* rev. ed. (Toronto: University of Toronto Press, 1996), 368.

14 Earle Birney, "Pacific Door," in *The Collected Poems of Earle Birney,* vol. 1 (Toronto: McClelland and Stewart, 1975), 141.

15 Robin Skelton, ed., introduction to *Six Poets of British Columbia* (Victoria: Sono Nis Press, 1980).

16 Thomas M. Sanford, "The Politics of Protest: The CCF and Social Credit League in British Columbia" (PhD thesis, University of California, Berkeley, 1961), 67. Martin Robin also used the "company province" metaphor in his study *The Rush to Spoils: The Company Province 1871-1933* (Toronto: McClelland and Stewart, 1972).

17 *British Columbia in the Canadian Confederation,* Submission to the Royal Commission on Dominion-Provincial Relations by the Government of British Columbia (Victoria, 1938), 23, 273, 276.

18 BC Ministry of Industry and Small Business Development, Preliminary figures for 1983.

19 "My government welcomes and fully supports the free trade agreement with the United States" – Lieutenant Governor R.G. Rogers, Speech from the Throne, BC, 34th Parliament, 2nd Session, 15 March 1988, 3456.

20 Government of British Columbia, *BC Media Handbook: Your Guide to British Columbia, Gateway to the Pacific Century* (1997), section 4, BC/APEC Trade, 3. See also Philip Resnick, "BC Capitalism and the Empire of the Pacific," *BC Studies* (Autumn 1985): 29-46.

21 Thus, Margaret Ormsby noted of the First World War: "With a population of less than 450,000, British Columbia contributed 55,570 men to Canada's war effort. Of this number, 43,202 served overseas; 6,225 lost their lives; and 13,607 were wounded" (Ormsby, *British Columbia,* 377).

22 John Norris, "Margaret Ormsby," in *Personality and History in British Columbia: Essays in Honour of Margaret Ormsby,* ed. Margaret Prang and John Norris (Vancouver, 1977), cited in Smith, *Canada: An American Nation?,* 291.

23 Walter Sage, "Geographical and Cultural Aspects of the Five Canadas," annual report of the Canadian Historical Association, 1937, cited in Smith, *Canada: An American Nation?,* 201.

24 Perhaps the most popular BC-directed film of recent years, Sandy Wilson's *My American Cousin,* recounts the coming of age in the slow-moving Okanagan Valley of the 1950s of a teenage girl enamoured of her American cousin with his red Cadillac convertible.

25 The figures are cited in J. Lewis Robinson and W.G. Hardwick, "The Canadian Cordillera," in *Canada: A Geographical Interpretation,* ed. John Warkentin (Toronto: Methuen, 1968), 467.

26 These data come from *BC Media Handbook,* Tab 4.

27 *BC Media Handbook,* Tab 2.

28 Alan Cairns, "Socialism, Federalism, and the BC Party System," in *Party Politics in Canada,* 5th ed., ed. Hugh Thorburn (Toronto: Prentice Hall, 1985), 300-1.

29 David Elkins, "British Columbia as a State of Mind," in *Two Political Worlds,* Donald Blake (Vancouver: UBC Press, 1985), 49.

30 Denny Boyd, "The Letters that Enrich Our Lives," *Vancouver Sun,* 1 May 1998,

discusses Harry Pick, who came to Canada from England in 1903 and wrote frequent letters to the *Sun* until his death in 1984.

31 Cited in Ormsby, *British Columbia,* 463.

32 Bruce Hutchison, *The Fraser* (Toronto: Clarke, Irwin, 1950), 189.

33 Edwin R. Black, "British Columbia: The Politics of Exploitation," in *Party Politics in Canada,* 4th ed., ed. Hugh Thorburn (Scarborough, ON: Prentice Hall, 1979), 294-5.

34 See Warren Magnusson et al., eds., *The New Reality* (Vancouver: New Star Books, 1984); Allen Garr, *Tough Guy: Bill Bennett and the Taking of British Columbia* (Toronto: Key Porter, 1985); Philip Resnick, "Neo-Conservatism on the Periphery: The Lessons from British Columbia," *BC Studies* (Autumn 1987): 3-23.

35 See Stuart Jamieson, *Times of Trouble: Labour Unrest and Industrial Conflict in Canada, 1900-1966,* Task Force on Labour Relations, Study 22 (Ottawa, 1966), for an excellent account of the roots of labour radicalism in BC.

36 See Ron McIsaac and Anne Champagne, eds., *Clayoquot Mass Trials: Defending the Rainforest* (Gabriola, BC: New Society Publishers, 1994).

37 See the discussion in Philip Resnick, "West Coast Blues. Why BC? Why PC?" *Inroads* 8 (1999): 179-91.

38 The percentages are based on data in Table A2-14, "Population of Canada by province, census data, 1851-1961," in M.C. Urquhart and K.A.M. Buckley, eds., *Historical Statistics of Canada* (Toronto: Macmillan, 1965), 14.

39 Diane Rinehart, "BC Boom Tops National Census," *Vancouver Sun,* 16 April 1997, A1, A3.

40 See Table 5.5, "Net Migration Flows 1961-1986," in David Bell, *The Roots of Disunity: A Study of Canadian Political Culture,* rev. ed. (Toronto: Oxford University Press, 1992), 133.

41 See Jim Sutherland, "Poll: Viewpoints Research Asked 700 of You Some Very Intimate Questions. Here Are Your Answers," *Vancouver Magazine,* December 1998, 56.

42 Gordon S. Galbraith, "British Columbia," in *The Provincial Political Systems,* ed. David Bellamy et al. (Toronto: Methuen, 1971), 65.

43 Cyril Belshaw, in *Transactions of the Thirteenth British Columbia Natural Resources Conference* (1961), 326.

44 Douglas Todd, "Poll Finds BC Least Religious," *Vancouver Sun,* 29 November 1996. A well-known BC writer, Douglas Coupland, entitled one of his short-story collections *Life after God* (New York: Pocketbooks, 1994).

45 The data come from a poll commissioned by Carleton University researchers and cited in Sutherland, "Poll," 62.

46 More than 70 percent of secular Canadians support free choice on abortion and homosexual rights; only 30 percent of committed evangelicals support the former and less than 40 percent the latter (Todd, "Poll Finds BC Least Religious").

47 In the 1970s, BC's divorce rate was the highest in Canada (Table 2.15, "Divorce Rates by Province," in *Perspectives Canada III* [Ottawa: Statistics Canada, 1980], 33). In 1996, BC, with about 13 percent of the Canadian population, accounted for more than 15 percent of all Canadian divorces (Table 6.1 in *Canada Year Book 1999* [Ottawa, 1998], 200).

48 British Columbia accounted for a full 25 percent of all drug offences in Canada in 1997 (*Canadian Crime Statistics* [Ottawa, 1997], 17, 37).

49 "Breaking and Entering in Canada," *Juristat* 18, no. 5 (1996): 4.

50 Sanford, "The Politics of Protest," 264. Interestingly enough, where suicide is concerned, BC is now in seventh place among Canada's provinces; Quebec has the dubious distinction of being in first place (Figure 6.27, "Suicide by Province," in *Births and Deaths* [Ottawa: Statistics Canada, 1995], 104).

51 Cited in Cernetig, *Far Side of the Rockies*, 452.

52 Cited in Sutherland, "Poll," 68.

53 Lewis Mumford, cited in Howard Odum and Harry Moore, eds., *American Regionalism: A Cultural-Historical Approach to National Integration* (New York: Henry Holt, 1938), 2.

54 Odum and Moore, *American Regionalism*, 16.

55 European Union, Committee of the Regions, *Regions and Cities, Pillars of Europe* (Amsterdam: European Union, 1997), 10.

56 Michael Keating, *The New Regionalism in Western Europe: Territorial Restructuring and Political Change* (Cheltenham, UK: Edward Elgar, 1998), 9.

57 Frances Halpenny, "The Humanities in Canada: A Study of Structure," in *Reinventing the Humanities: International Perspectives*, ed. David Myers (Kew: Australian Scholarly Publishers, 1995), 162. The term "limited identities" is itself associated with the article by the Canadian historian J.M.S. Careless, "Limited Identities in Canada," *Canadian Historical Review* 50 (1969): 1-10. My thanks to Allan Smith for pointing this out.

58 Robert Kroetsch, *The Lovely Treachery of Words*, cited in Seymour Martin Lipset, *Continental Divide* (London: Routledge, 1990), 209.

59 Michael Ornstein, "Regionalism and Canadian Political Ideology," in *Regionalism in Canada*, ed. Richard Brym, cited in Lipset, *Continental Divide*, 210.

60 Donald Smiley, *Canada in Question: Federalism in the Seventies* (Toronto: McGraw-Hill Ryerson, 1976), 196.

61 Alan Cairns, "The Governments and Societies of Canadian Federalism," in *Constitution, Government, and Society in Canada: Selected Essays* (Toronto: McClelland and Stewart, 1988), 145.

62 See Eric Hobsbawm and Terence Ranger, eds., *The Invention of Tradition* (Cambridge: Cambridge University Press, 1983). Benedict Anderson's well-known book is entitled *Imagined Communities: Reflections on the Origin and Spread of Nationalism*, rev. ed. (London: Verso, 1991), although he does not mean that the communities in question are invented out of naught.

63 "Ce qui frappe dans la Colombie c'est qu'elle forme comme une colonie de colonie" (Albert Métin, *La Colombie-Britannique* [Paris: Armand Colin, 1908], 391).

64 See Economic Council of Canada, *Living Together: A Study of Regional Disparities* (Ottawa, 1977), 35, for a table showing BC neck-and-neck with Ontario for first place in terms of personal income per capita by region between 1926 and 1975. When the data for Alberta are disaggregated from those of the other two Prairie provinces in recent decades, that province joins Ontario and BC at the top.

65 Michael Keating, *New Regionalism in Western Europe*, 187.

66 Kenichi Ohmae, *The End of the Nation State: The Rise of Regional Economies* (New York: Free Press, 1995), 79-80.

67 Thomas J. Courchene with Colin Telmer, *From Heartland to North American Region State: The Social, Fiscal and Federal Evolution of Ontario*, Faculty of Management, University of Toronto, Monograph Series on Public Policy (Toronto, 1998), 296, 304.

68 David Wolfe, "The Emergence of the Region State," in Thomas J. Courchene, ed., *The Nation State in a Global/Information Era: Policy Challenges* (Kingston, ON: Queen's University, John Deutsch Institute for the Study of Economic Policy, 1997), 207. Wolfe has somewhat retreated from his embrace of the region-state construct, as evidenced by his comments at a University of Toronto conference in March 1999 organized to discuss the Courchene thesis.

69 Norman J. Ruff, "Pacific Perspectives on the Canadian Confederation," in *Canada: The State of the Federation 1991*, ed. Douglas M. Brown (Kingston, ON: Queen's University, Institute for Intergovernmental Relations, 1991), 201.

70 Gordon Wilson, *A Civilized Revolution* (Vancouver: Ronsdale Press, 1996), 103.

71 Gordon Gibson, *Thirty Million Musketeers* (Vancouver: Fraser Institute/Key Porter, 1995), 203.

72 George Woodcock, *British Columbia: A History of the Province* (Vancouver: Douglas and McIntyre, 1990), 269.

73 Keating, *New Regionalism in Western Europe*, 3.

74 Henry Crease, cited in Derek Pethick, "The Confederation Debate of 1870," in *British Columbia and Confederation*, ed. George Shelton (Victoria: Morriss Printing, 1967), 169-70.

75 Louis Wirth, "Limitations of Regionalism," in *Regionalism in America*, ed. Merrill Jensen (Madison: University of Wisconsin Press, 1951), 391-2.

76 See the chapters on Italy and Belgium in Lieven de Winter and Huti Tusan, eds., *Regionalist Parties in Western Europe* (London: Routledge, 1998).

77 Luc Van den Brande, cited in Robert Owen, "Faultlines of the New Europe: Fragile States in Danger of Destruction," *The Times* (London), 29 December 1998.

78 Keating, *New Regionalism in Western Europe*, 108.

79 The phrase is cited in Bruce Hutchison, "From this Imperfect Moment, We Can Begin to Build," *Vancouver Sun*, 11 June 1990, A1.

80 "BC Opposes Equalization Payments," in George A. Rawlyk, Bruce Hodgins, and Richard Bowles, eds., *Regionalism in Canada: Flexible Federalism or Fractured Nation?* (Scarborough, ON: Prentice Hall, 1979), 47.

81 Vaughn Palmer, "Premier Satisfied with His Meech Stance," *Vancouver Sun*, 4 June 1990, A6.

82 Walter Sage, "Geographical and Cultural Aspects of the Five Canadas," annual report of the Canadian Historical Association, 1937, cited in Smith, *Canada: An American Nation?*, 259.

83 Bell, *The Roots of Disunity*, 146.

84 "In 1968, to the amusement of his fellow premiers and the federal cabinet, W.A.C. Bennett had unveiled a map that redefined Canada, with an enlarged British Columbia as one of five provinces. Each was to have equal representation in a Senate made up of provincial appointees" (Norman Ruff, "British Columbia and Canadian Federalism," in *The Reins of Power: Governing British*

Columbia, ed. Terence Morley et al. [Vancouver: Douglas and McIntyre, 1983], 301). See also David Mitchell, "BC's Biggest Constitutional Contribution? A Canada of Five Regions Has Been a Pursuit of Our Province for Most of This Century," *Vancouver Sun,* 19 December 1995, A15. Mitchell, however, dates Bennett's five-region map gambit from February 1969. He also notes that Premier Duff Pattullo had been promoting the notion of BC as one of Canada's five regions back in the 1930s – although obviously with less flair than W.A.C. Bennett was to show.

85 Cited in David Elton, "Federalism and the Canadian West," in *Perspectives on Canadian Federalism,* ed. R.D. Olling and M.M. Westmacott (Scarborough, ON: Prentice Hall, 1988), 357.

86 Keith Baldrey, "Recognition of All Canada's Regions as 'Distinct' Societies and an Elected Senate Are the Major Components of the BC Government's New Constitutional Plan Being Unveiled Today," *Vancouver Sun,* 23 January 1990, A1. Two federal Quebec cabinet ministers, Marcel Massé and Benoît Bouchard, rejected Vander Zalm's distinct society argument the next day. "British Columbia is different, Ontario is different, but not in the same way that Quebec is distinct," said Bouchard ("Scepticism Greets BC Plan for Meech," *Vancouver Sun,* 24 January 1990, A1). The exact wording of Vander Zalm's proposed clause would have involved recognizing Canada as a country "whose distinct national identity is founded upon and derives its strength from the unique characteristics of each of the provinces and territories" (Keith Baldrey, *Vancouver Sun,* 25 January 1990, A1).

87 Speaking notes for the Hon. Andrew Petter, Minister for Intergovernmental Affairs, Motion to the BC legislature on the Calgary Framework, 8.

88 From a 1963 speech cited in Paddy Sherman, *Bennett* (Toronto: McClelland and Stewart, 1966), 286.

89 "When [the Meech] accord died, Bill Vander Zalm said, the BC government got thousands of telephone calls from 'well-intentioned individuals,' nearly all of whom wanted to talk about why Canada always gives in to Quebec, or proclaim 'that we don't need Quebec ... we don't need the French'" (William Boei, "Premier Has New Doubts on Meech: Vander Zalm Says He Wouldn't Sign Pact if Faced with It Again," *Vancouver Sun,* 30 June 1990, A1).

90 Forty-seven percent of British Columbians surveyed mentioned concessions to Quebec as a major reason for disliking the Charlottetown Accord (Canada West Foundation, *Public Opinion and the Charlottetown Accord* [Calgary, January 1993], 4, reproduced in Roger Gibbins and Sonia Arrison, *Western Visions: Perspectives on the West in Canada* [Peterborough, ON: Broadview Press, 1995], 136). That same survey showed that only Albertans, at 54 percent, scored higher in their negative views of concessions to Quebec.

91 *Vancouver Sun,* 31 July 1997, reporting on the tabling of a report to the BC government by a panel headed by Gordon Wilson.

92 Ian Mulgrew, "Angry Carney Says BC Shouldn't Rule Out Separation," *Vancouver Sun,* 25 September 1997.

93 Gordon Gibson, *Globe and Mail,* 30 September 1997.

94 Peter O'Neil, *Vancouver Sun,* 20 December 1997.

95 Cernetig, "Far Side of the Rockies," 449.

96 "Nearly 90% of BC residents are opposed to their province becoming independent or joining the US if Quebec separates, a Viewpoints research survey found" ("BC Unimpressed by Separatism," *Globe and Mail,* 5 December 1995); "In BC, 91 per cent said that they didn't think the province 'should consider' becoming an independent country, while 88 per cent rejected the suggestion BC should consider joining the US" (Peter O'Neil, "BC Against Separation: Poll," *Vancouver Sun,* 25 April 1998).

97 See Table 10.6 in Maurice Pinard, Robert Bernier, and Vincent Lemieux, *Un combat inachevé* (Saint Foy: Presses de l'Université du Québec, 1997), 346. The 61 percent figure held true both in March 1995 and September 1996; 34 percent of respondents in 1995 were opposed to Quebec remaining a province of Canada and 31 percent in 1996.

98 Thus, a Decima/*Maclean's* survey in late 1989 showed that the first loyalty of 55 percent of Quebec respondents was to their province versus 44 percent whose first loyalty was to Canada; in British Columbia, 83 percent chose Canada first versus 17 percent who chose BC. Cited in David Kilgour, *Inside Outer Canada* (Edmonton: Lone Pine, 1990), 197.

99 *Citizens' Forum on Canada's Future* (Ottawa: Minister of Supply and Services, 1991), 54.

100 Ibid., 47.

101 David Elkins, "Allegiance and Discontent in British Columbia," in Blake, *Two Political Worlds,* 131.

102 Gibbins and Arrison, *Western Visions,* 111.

103 Interestingly, Pat McGeer, a former Social Credit cabinet minister as well as former leader of the BC Liberal Party, called for the creation of a British Columbia Party to pursue BC's own constitutional objectives in a 1990 op-ed article, "Standing Behind Regional Strength," *Vancouver Sun,* 23 May 1990, A13. Even McGeer, however, stopped short of setting sovereignty as his objective, talking instead of moving Canada towards a Swiss-type model, "where the national government is largely financed by the cantons." There were few takers for McGeer's proposal.

104 Dave Barrett, then leader of the opposition, stated the following during a debate in April 1980: "The continuation of the present program of healthcare and hospital care on a Canada-wide basis is essential to the well-being of all Canadians and to Canadian unity. To allow these services to be eroded would add fuel to the fires of those who seek to divide Canada. One of British Columbia's major concerns, aside from maintaining a level of its own services, is to avoid taking a position or agreeing to an arrangement that might balkanize the country" (BC, 32nd Parliament, 2nd Session, 16 April 1980, 2010).

105 See the findings of a December 1998 Angus Reid poll reporting that 63 percent of respondents in BC favoured the right of provinces to opt out of national programs as long as they provided a similar program of their own, but also that 55 percent of respondents in BC (versus 47 percent in Canada as a whole) agree that Ottawa alone should enforce national standards (*Globe and Mail,* 23 December 1998, 1, 7).

106 "A Dominion of British Columbia," *Vancouver Sun,* 14 May 1934, cited in Rawlyk et al., *Regionalism in Canada,* 142-4. This front-page editorial concludes:

"If we are forced to it by eastern Canada, we can separate and pay our own way and go alone; and we can be sure we will have 100% British support ... There must be a more equitable sharing among Canadians of things Canadian, or else the province must look about in self-defence to find ways and means to federate these parts into a Dominion of British Columbia."

107 Donald Stainsby, from an article in *Saturday Night* in April 1964, reprinted in Rawlyk et al., *Regionalism in Canada,* 45.

108 Bruce Hutchison, *The Unknown Country* (Toronto: Longmans, Green, 1948), 275, cited in Ruff, "Pacific Perspectives on the Canadian Confederation," 201.

109 As one observer, among many, notes: "As in any very large and sparsely populated land, people here characteristically identify with their own specific region. Each region, geographically unique, predetermines a certain way of life. For example, the Cariboo-Chilcotin region immediately evokes images of vast, rolling landscape and a difficult, frontier existence. A regional approach to BC not only helps gain an understanding of this vast province, it accurately reflects the character of the people and the geography" (Ted Wrinkle, *British Columbia: BC Photographs* [Portland, OR: Beautiful West Publishing], 8).

110 Robert White-Harvey, "Why Vancouver Island Should Go It Alone," *Globe and Mail,* 14 March 1998, D9.

111 See "Vancouver Secedes: You Read It Here First," *Vancouver Magazine,* theme issue edited by Douglas Coupland, October 1997.

112 Nonetheless, Cascadia has its adherents. See Ian Gill, "A Green Island in a Sea of Envy: Welcome to Cascadia," *Georgia Straight,* 5-12 June 1992, 7-9; Michael Goldberg and Maurice Levi, "The Evolving Experience along the Pacific Northwest Corridor Called Cascadia," *New Pacific,* Winter 1992/3, 28-32; Cascadia Border Bi-National Pilot Project, Discovery Institute, Seattle, 1994; Graham Fysh, "Banking on Cascadia," *New Pacific,* January 1994, 52-4; Barbara Yaffe, "Cascadia Is Sometimes a Great Notion, but It Falters on Practical Grounds," *Vancouver Sun,* 16 August 1997. A slightly different twist on the same argument is associated with the idea of Ecotopia, a region spanning Alaska, BC, Washington, Oregon, and northern California; see Ernest Callenbach, *Ecotopia* (Berkeley: Banyan Tree Books, 1975); Joel Garreau, *The Nine Nations of North America* (Boston: Houghton Mifflin, 1981).

113 *Montreal Gazette* writer Paul Wells, cited in Barbara Yaffe, "Quebecers No More 'A People' than Are British Columbians," *Vancouver Sun,* 4 December 1997, A14.

114 Perhaps the most intelligent reflection on the contemporary meaning of these two terms is that of the eminent Italian political philosopher Norberto Bobbio, who notes that the major distinction between right and left ultimately comes down to "a different perception of what makes human beings equal and what makes them unequal" (Norberto Bobbio, *Left and Right: The Significance of a Political Distinction* [University of Chicago Press, 1996], 69).

115 Jean Bethke Elshtain, *Democracy on Trial* (Concord, ON: Anansi, 1993).

116 See Charles Taylor, *The Malaise of Modernity* (Concord, ON: Anansi, 1991); also *Reconciling the Solitudes* (Montreal: McGill-Queen's University Press, 1993), chap. 8.

117 Ernest Gellner, *Nationalism* (London: Weidenfeld and Nicolson, 1997), 94.

118 Ibid., 96.

Chapter 2: BC Political Leaders and Canadian Unity

1 Premier W.A.C. Bennett, speaking to a Social Credit convention in New Westminster, cited in Paddy Sherman, *Bennett* (Toronto: McClelland and Stewart, 1966), 285-6.

2 Premier W.A.C. Bennett, Opening Statement of the Province of British Columbia to the Federal-Provincial Conference, Ottawa, 15-17 November 1971, 8-9.

3 Premier William R. Bennett, Speech to the Montreal Board of Trade, 12 May 1980, 11, 13, 15.

4 Premier Mike Harcourt, cited in Patrick Nagle, "Separatists' 'global pretensions' offend BC," *Vancouver Sun,* 19 May 1994.

5 Premier William R. Bennett, Speech to the Montreal Board of Trade, 12 May 1980, 9.

6 Premier Bill Vander Zalm, cited in Doug Ward, "Vander Zalm Steps into Meech Lake Fray," *Vancouver Sun,* 18 January 1990.

7 Gordon Campbell, Leader of the Opposition, cited by Barbara Yaffe, *Vancouver Sun,* 18 November 1995.

8 Premier Glen Clark, cited by Barbara Yaffe, *Vancouver Sun,* 20 February 1996.

9 Premier David Barrett, Opening Statement of the Province of British Columbia to the Federal-Provincial Conference, Ottawa, 23-25 May 1973, 1.

10 Premier William R. Bennett, Speech to the Montreal Board of Trade, 12 May 1980, 8.

11 Transcript of a TV Address by Premier Bill Vander Zalm, 28 May 1990.

12 Hon. Andrew Petter, Motion to the BC Legislature on the Calgary Framework, 19 May 1998, 3.

13 Premier William R. Bennett, Speech to the Montreal Board of Trade, 12 May 1980, 9.

14 Premier Glen Clark, cited by Barbara Yaffe, *Vancouver Sun,* 20 February 1996.

15 Bill Vander Zalm, cited in Neale Adams, "Facing BC Separatism," *Vancouver Sun,* 12 March 1977.

16 Premier Glen Clark, cited by Barbara Yaffe, *Vancouver Sun,* 6 September 1996.

17 Pat Carney, cited by Barbara Yaffe, *Vancouver Sun,* 18 December 1997.

18 Premier William R. Bennett, Speech to Federal-Provincial Conference, Ottawa, December 1976.

19 Opening Remarks by Premier Rita Johnston, 32nd Annual Premiers' Conference, Whistler, BC, 26-27 August 1991, 5.

20 Moe Sihota, Minister of Constitutional Affairs, cited in Vaughn Palmer, "NDP on the Side of Expedient Resolution," *Vancouver Sun,* 27 January 1992, A12.

21 Premier Mike Harcourt's statement on the Quebec referendum, 30 October 1995, 5.

22 Andrew Petter, Minister of Intergovernmental Affairs, Speech to Investment Dealers of Canada, Whistler, BC, 16 June 1997, 6.

23 Andrew Petter, Minister of Intergovernmental Affairs, cited by Barbara Yaffe, *Vancouver Sun,* 12 October 1996.

24 Premier W.A.C. Bennett, British Columbia's Proposals to the Working Session of First Ministers on Non-Constitutional Matters, Ottawa, 16 September 1970.

25 Barrett, Opening Statement of the Province of British Columbia, 23-25 May 1973, 2.

26 Premier William R. Bennett, Opening Statement to the Federal-Provincial Conference of First Ministers, Ottawa, 14-15 June 1976, 5.

27 Premier William Vander Zalm, Opening Statement to the First Ministers' Conference, Vancouver, 20-21 November 1986, 4-6.

28 There is a discussion of this proposed measure in Gary Mason and Keith Baldrey, *Fantasyland: Inside the Reign of Bill Vander Zalm* (Toronto: McGraw-Hill Ryerson, 1989). See also Vaughn Palmer, "Premier Could Be Separatist, Book Claims," *Vancouver Sun,* 6 November 1989, A12.

29 Hon. Andrew Petter, Presentation to Special Senate Committee on Bill C-110, Ottawa, 23 January 1996, 3-4.

30 See David Mitchell, "BC's Biggest Constitutional Contribution? A Canada of Five Regions Has Been a Pursuit of the Province for Most of This Century," *Vancouver Sun,* 19 December 1995, A15.

31 Premier Bill Bennett, Speech to the Men's Canadian Club of Vancouver, 17 May 1978, 20-2; Opening Remarks by Premier William R. Bennett to Federal-Provincial Conference of First Ministers, Ottawa, 30 October to 1 November 1978, 10.

32 See Vaughn Palmer, "Mr. Chrétien Knows How to Unite BC, if not Canada," *Vancouver Sun,* 28 November 1995; Justine Hunter, "BC Gets Short End of the Stick from Ottawa," *Vancouver Sun,* 9 December 1995, A18.

33 Hon. Andrew Petter, Presentation to Special Senate Committee on Bill C-110, Ottawa, 23 January 1996, 2-3.

34 Cited in Bruce Hutchison, "From this Imperfect Moment, We Can Begin to Build," *Vancouver Sun,* 11 June 1990, A1.

35 Premier Bill Bennett, cited in Stanley Meisler, "Us, as Seen by One of Them: An American's Look at BC," *Vancouver Sun,* 15 May 1980.

36 Gordon Campbell, cited in Miro Cernetig, "Blue Grit," *Globe and Mail Report on Business Magazine,* April 1996, 90.

37 Premier Glen Clark, cited by Barbara Yaffe, *Vancouver Sun,* 6 September 1996.

38 Pat Carney, transcript of comments to BC Unity Panel, Vancouver, 16 December 1997.

39 Opening Statement of the Province of British Columbia to the Federal-Provincial Conference of First Ministers, Ottawa, 9-10 April 1975, 4.

40 Hon. William R. Bennett, Remarks to the First Ministers' Conference on the Economy, Regina, 14 February 1985, 3.

41 Opening Statement by Premier William Vander Zalm to the First Ministers' Conference, Toronto, 24-27 November 1987, 9.

42 Premier Mike Harcourt, cited by Vaughn Palmer, *Vancouver Sun,* 15 October 1992.

43 Premier Glen Clark, cited in Edward Greenspon and Graham Fraser, "PM Finds More Cash to Woo Provinces: On Eve of Talks with Premiers, He Prepares to Sweeten Health Offer," *Globe and Mail,* 3 February 1999, A1.

44 An Address by Premier W.A.C. Bennett to the Canadian Chamber of Commerce, Vancouver, 12 September 1962, 6, 8.

45 British Columbia's proposals to the Working Session of First Ministers on Non-Constitutional Matters, Ottawa, 16 September 1970, 1-2.

46 British Columbia's Proposals on Income Security in Canada, Federal-Provincial Conference of First Ministers, Ottawa, 23-25 May 1973, 8.

47 Premier David Barrett, Opening Statement of the Province of British Columbia to the Federal-Provincial Conference, Ottawa, 23-25 May 1973, 2.

48 Ibid., 8.

49 Opening Statement of the Province of British Columbia to the Federal-Provincial First Ministers' Conference on Energy, Ottawa, 22-23 January 1974, 1.

50 Premier William R. Bennett, Speech to the Montreal Board of Trade, 12 May 1980, 3.

51 Premier William R. Bennett, Towards an Economic Strategy for Canada: The British Columbia Position, February 1978, 27; Premier William R. Bennett, Notes for Remarks on the Public Sector, Federal-Provincial Conference of First Ministers, Ottawa, 13-15 February 1978, 4.

52 Bennett, Towards an Economic Strategy, 36-7.

53 Premier William R. Bennett, Statement to Federal-Provincial Conference on the Economy, Ottawa, February 1982, 9.

54 Premier William R. Bennett, Opening Statement to Annual Conference of First Ministers, Halifax, 28-29 November 1985, 3.

55 Hon. William R. Bennett, Remarks to the First Ministers' Conference on the Economy, Regina, 14 February 1985, 8.

56 Bennett, Towards an Economic Strategy, 40.

57 Premier William Vander Zalm, Opening Statement to the First Ministers' Conference, Vancouver, 20-21 November 1986, 2.

58 Premier William Vander Zalm, Opening Statement to First Ministers' Conference on Aboriginal Constitutional Matters, Ottawa, 25-27 March 1987.

59 Premier William Vander Zalm, Statement to the First Ministers' Conference on Economic Development, Toronto, 26-27 November 1987, 5.

60 Premier William Vander Zalm, Opening Statement, Annual Conference of First Ministers, Ottawa, 9-10 November 1989.

61 See Vaughn Palmer, "Premier Satisfied with His Meech Stance," *Vancouver Sun,* 4 June 1990, A6.

62 Keith Baldrey, *Vancouver Sun,* 23 and 25 January 1990.

63 Transcript of an Address by Premier William Vander Zalm, 17 January 1990, 7.

64 Transcript of a TV Address by Premier William Vander Zalm, 28 May 1990, 7.

65 Premier Mike Harcourt, Address to the Canadian Chamber of Commerce, Victoria, 28 September 1992, 1, 3, 4.

66 Premier's Statement on Quebec Referendum, 30 October 1995, 5.

67 Glen Clark, cited by Barbara Yaffe, *Vancouver Sun,* 13 September 1997.

68 Glen Clark, cited by Barbara Yaffe, *Vancouver Sun,* 16 September 1997.

69 Andrew Petter, cited by Barbara Yaffe, *Vancouver Sun,* 12 October 1996.

70 Andrew Petter, cited by Barbara Yaffe, *Vancouver Sun,* 4 October 1996.

71 Hon. Andrew Petter, Motion to the BC Legislature on the Calgary Framework, 19 May 1998, 8.

72 Sherman, *Bennett,* 298.

73 See the discussion in Frances Russell, "Victoria's Shameful Separatism Show," *Vancouver Sun,* 24 January 1977.

74 Marjorie Nichols, "Greed Addles the Socred Brains," *Vancouver Sun,* 22 July 1980.

75 Peter O'Neil, "We'll Help BC to Separate, Wilson Pledges," *Vancouver Sun,* 29 April 1994, B3.

76 Gordon Gibson, *Renewing the Federation: Options for British Columbia* (Victoria: Queen's Printer for British Columbia, 1997), 36-7.
77 Ian Mulgrew, "Angry Carney Says BC Shouldn't Rule Out Separation," *Vancouver Sun,* 25 September 1997.
78 Cited in Sherman, *Bennett,* 299.
79 Cited in Russell, "Victoria's Shameful Separatism Show."
80 "Bennett Hits at Separatism," *Vancouver Sun,* 6 November 1980.
81 Alan Twigg, *Vander Zalm: From Immigrant to Premier* (Madeira Park, BC: Harbour Publishing, 1986), 239.
82 Bill Vander Zalm, cited in Keith Baldrey, "BC Seeks Greater Economic Autonomy," *Vancouver Sun,* 9 June 1990.
83 Vaughn Palmer, "Premier Could Be Separatist, Book Claims," *Vancouver Sun,* 6 November 1989, A12. Palmer cites Gary Mason and Keith Baldrey, two *Vancouver Sun* reporters who had authored a book on Bill Vander Zalm entitled *Fantasyland* (Toronto: McGraw-Hill Ryerson, 1989) and who had had access to the premier's two top aides, Bob Ransford and David Poole. The first aide is reported to have asked the second, "Does the premier want to separate?" To which the second replied, "Oh, you'd be surprised how far he would go."
84 Glen Clark, cited by Barbara Yaffe, *Vancouver Sun,* 20 February 1996.
85 Andrew Petter, cited by Barbara Yaffe, *Vancouver Sun,* 2 August 1997.
86 David J. Mitchell, *WAC: Bennett and the Rise of British Columbia* (Vancouver: Douglas and McIntyre, 1983), 351.
87 Opening Remarks by Premier William R. Bennett to Federal-Provincial Conference of First Ministers, Ottawa, 30 October to 1 November 1978, 6, 10.
88 Premier William R. Bennett, Speech to the Montreal Board of Trade, 12 May 1980, 5.
89 Premier William Vander Zalm, Opening Statement to the First Ministers' Conference, Vancouver, 20-21 November 1986, 4; Transcript of a TV Address by Premier William Vander Zalm, 28 May 1990, 12.
90 Transcript of a TV Address by Premier William Vander Zalm, 28 May 1990, 6.
91 Gordon Wilson, *A Civilized Revolution* (Vancouver: Ronsdale Press, 1996), 107.
92 Andrew Petter, cited by Barbara Yaffe, *Vancouver Sun,* 10 October 1997.
93 Hon. Andrew Petter, Motion to the BC Legislature on the Calgary Framework, 19 May 1998, 8.
94 Canada, "Constitutional Conference Proceedings," Second meeting, Ottawa, 10-12 February 1969, 86, cited by Stephen Tomblin, *Ottawa and the Outer Provinces: The Challenge of Regional Integration in Canada* (Toronto: Lorimer, 1995), 151.
95 Cited in Sherman, *Bennett,* 298.
96 Premier William R. Bennett, Opening Statement to the Federal-Provincial Conference of First Ministers, Ottawa, 14-15 June 1978.
97 Premier William R. Bennett, First Ministers' Conference, Ottawa, 1980.
98 Hon. Garde Gardom, Speaking notes to the Osler Society, Vancouver, 11 May 1981, 4.
99 John Reynolds, MLA, BC Hansard, 33rd Parliament, 1st Session, 8 July 1983, 182.
100 Bill Vander Zalm, cited in Baldrey, "BC Seeks Greater Economic Autonomy."
101 Peter O'Neil, "Harcourt Called the Laughing Stock of Ottawa Conference,"

Vancouver Sun, 24 August 1992; Carol Goar, "Some Bargainers Did a Bit Better than Others. Mike Harcourt, Unfortunately, Wasn't Among Them," reprinted in the *Vancouver Sun,* 25 August 1992, A11; Vaughn Palmer, "Harcourt Goofed and that's a Problem," *Vancouver Sun,* 25 August 1992, A10.

102 Mike Harcourt and Wayne Skene, *Harcourt: A Measure of Defiance* (Vancouver: Douglas and McIntyre, 1996), 35.

103 B.C. Unity Panel, Transcript of Meeting with the Premier, Vancouver, 16 December 1997.

104 Barbara Yaffe, "Would-be Premier Wants BC Recognized as 'Different,'" *Vancouver Sun,* 18 November 1995.

105 Prime Minister Pierre Trudeau, cited in Patrick Nagle, "Drop Petty Gripes, Trudeau Tells BC," *Vancouver Sun,* 25 November 1981. Trudeau was referring to the fact that British Columbians were fixated on local, at the expense of national, politics.

106 Jean Chrétien, cited in A. Wilson-Smith and Edward Greenspon, *Double Vision: The Inside Story of the Liberals in Power,* cited in Barbara Yaffe, "New Book Emphasizes Distance Between BC and PMO," *Vancouver Sun,* 24 October 1996.

107 This is precisely the argument that Roger Gibbins, director of the Canada West Foundation, Calgary, advanced in a conversation with the author on 26 July 1999, and it is one with which I concur.

Chapter 3: BC Opinion-Makers and Canadian Unity

1 See Philip Resnick, "Whatever Happened to Civil Society?" chap. 7 in *Twenty-First Century Democracy* (Montreal: McGill-Queen's University Press, 1997).

2 Rafe Mair, *Canada: Is Anyone Listening?* (Toronto: Key Porter, 1998), 141, 225.

3 Rafe Mair, Brief to BC Unity Panel, 16 December 1997.

4 Melvin H. Smith, *The Renewal of the Federation: A British Columbia Perspective* (Victoria: Queen's Printer for British Columbia, 1991), 48, 52.

5 Cyril Shelford, "Canada's Future," in *Discussion Papers on British Columbia in Confederation* (Victoria: Queen's Printer for British Columbia, 1991), 79.

6 Pat McGeer, *Vancouver Sun,* 15 October 1992, A21.

7 Ted Byfield, "Why Can't the Rest of Us Put Limits on Quebec's Referendum Habit?" *British Columbia Report,* 12 September 1994, 44.

8 "Secessionists Inflict Racism on Canadians," *Vancouver Sun,* 14 March 1998, A22.

9 "A Reality Check for the Parti Québécois," *Vancouver Sun,* 2 December 1998, A18.

10 Cited in Barbara Yaffe, "Potential for 'Creative Compromise' on Unity Slipping Away," *Vancouver Sun,* 26 October 1996, A3.

11 Cited in Barbara Yaffe, *Vancouver Sun,* 22 August 1996.

12 Cited in Barbara Yaffe, "New Minister Singing the Same Old 'Distinct-Society' Tune," *Vancouver Sun,* 6 March 1996, A3.

13 Cited in Barbara Yaffe, *Vancouver Sun,* 11 September 1996.

14 Gordon Gibson, *Thirty Million Musketeers* (Toronto: Key Porter, 1995), 1.

15 Cited in Barbara Yaffe, "Two Letter-Writing Lawyers Trying to Bridge Two Solitudes," *Vancouver Sun,* 16 December 1996, A3.

16 Cited in Miro Cernetig, "The Yin and Yang of BC Nationalism," *Globe and Mail,* 27 September 1997, D2.

17 Business Council of BC, "The Future of Canada: A BC Business Perspective," 13 February 1992, 5.

18 Vancouver Board of Trade, "Future of the Federation and Unity of Canada," Discussion paper, 5 March 1997, 27.

19 Ron Burns, "The Course of True Love Never Did Run Smooth," *Discussion Papers on British Columbia in Confederation* (Victoria: Queen's Printer for British Columbia, 1991), 10.

20 Robert Clark, "With Our Nation in Peril, What Should British Columbia Do?" in *Discussion Papers on British Columbia in Confederation* (Victoria: Queen's Printer for British Columbia, 1991), 17.

21 Canadian Jewish Congress, Pacific Region, Brief to the BC Unity Panel, 23 December 1997.

22 See, for example, "Amen, Mr. Premier," *Vancouver Sun*, 15 February 1990, A14, praising Bill Vander Zalm for speaking out in favour of the Meech Lake Accord; "Wilson Blunders into No-Man's-Land," *Vancouver Sun*, 25 September 1992, criticizing Gordon Wilson, then leader of the BC Liberal Party, for coming out against the Charlottetown Accord; "Unity Panel Needs a Francophone," *Vancouver Sun*, 4 November 1997, favouring the appointment of a francophone to the BC Unity Panel and the larger purpose behind the Calgary Declaration, namely, "to reknit the Canadian fabric."

23 Vaughn Palmer, *Vancouver Sun*, 12 June 1990.

24 Tom Berger, "English Canada and Quebec's Rendezvous with Independence," in *Discussion Papers on British Columbia in Confederation* (Victoria: Queen's Printer for British Columbia, 1991), 2-3, 6.

25 Transcript of meeting with the BC Unity Panel, 16 December 1997.

26 BC Teachers' Federation, Brief to the BC Unity Panel, December 1997, 4.

27 Angus Reid, cited in Cernetig, "Yin and Yang of BC Nationalism," D1.

28 Gibson, *Thirty Million Musketeers*, 237.

29 Berger, "English Canada and Quebec's Rendezvous," 3.

30 Editorial, *Vancouver Sun*, 16 December 1997.

31 David Mitchell, cited by Barbara Yaffe, *Vancouver Sun*, 6 March 1996.

32 Gibson, *Thirty Million Musketeers*, 18, 156, 158.

33 Ibid., 189. Gibson makes the same argument in his study *Renewing the Federation: BC and Canadian Unity* (Victoria: Queen's Printer for British Columbia, 1997), 77.

34 Smith, *Renewal of the Federation*, ii.

35 Ibid., 11.

36 Ibid., 26.

37 Walter Hardwick, "Re-ordering Canada," in *Discussion Papers on British Columbia in Confederation* (Victoria: Queen's Printer for British Columbia, 1991), 50.

38 Business Council of BC, "The Future of Canada," 4.

39 George Koch, "Confederation in Crisis," *British Columbia Report*, 29 January 1990, 17.

40 Tex Enemark, "Constitutional Reform: A Radical BC Proposal," in *Discussion Papers on British Columbia in Confederation* (Victoria: Queen's Printer for British Columbia, 1991), 30.

41 David Elkins, cited by Jamie Lamb, *Vancouver Sun*, 29 April 1982.

42 Miro Cernetig, "The Far Side of the Rockies: Politics and Identity in British

Columbia," in *A Passion for Identity,* ed. David Taras and Beverley Rasporich (Toronto: Nelson, 1997), 460-1.

43 Editorial, *Vancouver Sun,* 9 January 1999.

44 Cited by Barbara Yaffe, *Vancouver Sun,* 23 August 1997.

45 Cited in Miro Cernetig, "The Yin and Yang of BC Nationalism," *Globe and Mail,* 27 September 1997.

46 Bruce Hutchison, *Vancouver Sun,* 5 April 1980.

47 Berger, "English Canada and Quebec's Rendezvous," 1.

48 Burns, "The Course of True Love," 8.

49 Clark, "With Our Nation in Peril," 20, 23.

50 Editorial, *Vancouver Sun,* 6 February 1991, A12.

51 Cited in Barbara Yaffe, "No One Is Leading the Charge in BC for a Better Vision of a United Canada," *Vancouver Sun,* 23 August 1997, A3.

52 See, for example, Claude Ryan's quite telling piece "The Agreement on the Canadian Social Union as Seen by a Quebec Federalist," *Inroads,* no. 8 (1999): 25-41. He argues: "In the case of the spending power, [any] approach should take into consideration the fact that Quebec is considerably different and should be given the right to withdraw unconditionally from all Canada-wide programs within provincial jurisdiction. This withdrawal should be accompanied by financial compensation in the form of either cash or tax transfers" (p. 40).

53 See, for example, *BC Media Handbook,* a glossy publication of over 100 pages with tables and charts, distributed to the thousands of media representatives attending the November 1997 APEC summit in Vancouver. It uses the phrase "British Columbia Gateway to the Pacific Century" on the cover and on the table of contents for each of the five subsections that make up the volume.

54 Thomas A. Hutton, *The Transformation of Canada's Pacific Metropolis: A Study of Vancouver* (Montreal: Institute for Research on Public Policy, 1998), 10-11.

55 Michael Kan, cited in Tom Fennell and Frances Kelly, "The Right Stuff?" *Maclean's,* Special Issue British Columbia, 24 August 1992, 33.

56 George Woodcock, *British Columbia: A History of the Province* (Vancouver: Douglas and McIntyre, 1990), 269.

57 Hardwick, "Re-ordering Canada," 50.

58 David Mitchell, *Vancouver Sun,* 1 August 1996.

59 Lisa Birnie Hobbs, "The West Coast: A Unique Land with a Powerful Sense of Newness," *Vancouver Sun,* 10 August 1996.

60 Jerry Pethick, "Visions in the Blood," *Capilano Review* (Fall 1989): 97-9, cited in Laurie Ricou, "The Writing of British Columbia Writing," *BC Studies* (Winter 1993-94): 107.

61 David Ablett, *Vancouver Sun,* 11 February 1977.

62 Ronald Shearer, "The Economy," *BC Studies* (Winter 1993-94): 138.

63 T. Barnes, D. Edgington, K. Denike, and T. McGee, "Vancouver, the Province, and the Pacific Rim," in *Vancouver and Its Region,* ed. G. Wynn and T. Oke (Vancouver: UBC Press, 1992), 187.

64 Hutton, *Transformation of Canada's Pacific Metropolis,* 152-7.

65 See Peter Ward, *White Canada Forever: Popular Attitudes and Public Policy Toward Orientals in British Columbia* (Montreal: McGill-Queen's University Press, 1978), for but one exploration of this theme.

66 "BC Has Embraced the Larger World All Canada Seeks," *Vancouver Sun*, 28 October 1995, A22.
67 David Mitchell, "Our Multicultural Ethos Makes BC Unique Among Provinces," *Vancouver Sun*, 1 August 1996, A11.
68 Douglas Coupland, "Vancouver: Our Future," *Vancouver Magazine*, October 1997, 52.
69 Cited in Cernetig, "Yin and Yang of BC Nationalism," D2.
70 Adrian Dorst and Cameron Young, *Clayoquot: On the Wild Side* (Vancouver: Western Canada Wilderness Committee, 1990), reproduced in *Clayoquot Mass Trials: Defending the Rainforest*, ed. Ron McIsaac and Anne Champagne (Gabriola, BC: New Society Publishers, 1994), 3-4.
71 Cited in James Deacon, "Green Cathedrals: BC Tourism Enjoys a Backcountry Boom," *Maclean's*, 24 August 1992, 53.
72 Don Blake, Neil Guppy, and Peter Urmetzer, "Being Green in BC: Public Attitudes Towards Environmental Issues," *BC Studies* (Winter 1996-97): 59-60.
73 Vaughn Palmer, *Vancouver Sun*, 27 October 1992.
74 Hobbs, "The West Coast."
75 Cited in Tom Barrett, "BC Will Be the Tough Background," *Vancouver Sun*, 19 September 1992.
76 Cited by Tim Gallagher, *British Columbia Report*, 5 February 1990, 7.
77 David Elkins, "Politics as a Canadian Game," *BC Studies* (Winter 1993-94): 48, 52-55.
78 Cole Harris, *The Resettlement of British Columbia* (Vancouver: UBC Press, 1997), 274-5.
79 Editorial, *BC Studies* (Autumn/Winter 1997-98): 4.
80 Rebecca Bateman, "Comparative Thoughts on the Politics of Aboriginal Assimilation," *BC Studies* (Summer 1997): 81.
81 James Tully, *Strange Multiplicity: Constitutionalism in an Age of Diversity* (Cambridge: Cambridge University Press, 1995), 17.
82 Terry Glavin, cited in Daniel Gawthrop, *Highwire Act: Power, Pragmatism, and the Harcourt Legacy* (Vancouver: New Star Books, 1996), 233.
83 Mel Smith, from a speech to the Vancouver Board of Trade, cited in Gerald Friesen, *The West: Regional Ambitions, National Debates, Global Age* (Toronto: Penguin, 1999), 77-8.
84 Terry Morley, *Vancouver Sun*, 20 December 1997, A21, cited in Friesen, *The West*, 79.
85 Gordon Gibson, "A Principled Analysis of the Nisga'a Treaty," *Inroads*, no. 8 (1999): 163-78.
86 Alma Howard, "British Columbia and Canada's Future," in *Discussion Papers on British Columbia in Confederation* (Victoria: Queen's Printer for British Columbia, 1991), 56.
87 Paul Tennant, "Aboriginal Peoples and Aboriginal Title in British Columbia Politics," in *Politics, Policy, and Government in British Columbia*, ed. R.K. Carty (Vancouver: UBC Press, 1996), 63-4.
88 Robert Fulford, "Dream Country," *Vancouver Sun*, 14 January 1976.
89 Cited in Kevin Doyle, "Where the Sun Shines Best," *Maclean's*, 24 August 1992, 4.
90 Roderick Haig-Brown, "British Columbia: Loggers and Lotus Eaters," in *Canada:*

A Guide to the Peaceable Kingdom, ed. William Kilbourn (Toronto: Macmillan, 1970), 128.

91 Hobbs, "The West Coast."

92 Justine Brown, "Nowherelands: Utopian Communities in BC Fiction," *BC Studies* (Spring 1996): 6, 27.

93 Jack Hodgins, ed., "Introduction," in *The West Coast Experience* (Toronto: Macmillan, 1976), 2.

94 Coupland, "Vancouver: Our Future," 52.

95 Jean Barman, *The West beyond the West: A History of British Columbia,* rev. ed. (Toronto: University of Toronto Press, 1996), 353, 368.

96 Gawthrop, *Highwire Act,* 350.

97 Allan Fotheringham, "Smelling Flowers in the Slow Lane," *Maclean's,* 24 August 1992, 64.

98 Peter Newman, "Essay," *Maclean's,* 24 August 1992, 13.

99 Jamie Lamb, *Vancouver Sun,* 15 March 1982.

100 Robin Skelton, "Night Poem, Vancouver Island," in *Contemporary Poetry of British Columbia,* ed. Michael Yates (Victoria: Sono Nis Press, 1970), 1.

101 Earle Birney, "David," in *The Collected Poems of Earle Birney,* vol. 1 (Toronto: McClelland and Stewart, 1975), 108.

102 Russell McDougall, "The Anxiety of Influence: Literary Regionalism in the Canadian and Australian West," *World Literature Written in English* 25 (1985): 151-60, cited in Ricou, "Writing of British Columbia Writing," 106.

103 bill bissett, "Interview with Maidie Hilmo," *Essays on Canadian Writing* 32 (1986): 134-46, cited in Ricou, "Writing of British Columbia Writing," 107.

104 Tom Berger, "Among Quebec's Distinctions Is Its Struggle for Its Identity," *Vancouver Sun,* 24 October 1997.

105 Woodcock, *British Columbia,* 269.

106 Pat McGeer, "Pitching the BC Party. Canada Doesn't Need Grovelling Junior Partners to Placate Quebec. Canada Needs a Regional Rejuvenation, a Renewal of a Partnership of Equals," *Vancouver Sun,* 23 May 1990, A13.

107 Gibson, *Thirty Million Musketeers,* 49.

108 Vaughn Palmer, *Vancouver Sun,* 26 September 1991, A18.

109 Moira Farrow, "Provincial Governments Are the Villains," *Vancouver Sun,* 30 June 1980.

110 See the brief discussion of Gellner's views on nationalism at the end of Chapter 1.

111 Bruce Hutchison, "Surrender of Separatism," in *British Columbia: A Centennial Anthology,* ed. Reginald E. Watters (Toronto: McClelland and Stewart, 1958), 456.

112 Doug Christie, cited in David Wright, "On the Fringe," *Vancouver Sun,* 19 November 1976.

113 "Independent BC Advocated," *Vancouver Sun,* 13 October 1981.

114 George Woodcock, *Confederation Betrayed: The Case against Trudeau's Canada* (Madeira Park, BC: Harbour Publishing, 1981), 12.

115 *Vancouver Sun,* 25 October 1980.

116 Cited in Richard Gwyn, "West's Alienation Growing into Separatism," *Vancouver Sun,* 19 February 1977.

117 Charles Hayes, "The Henpecked Revolutionary. Secede, Says the Okanagan's Fred Washburn," *British Columbia Report,* 26 February 1990, 44.

118 *Vancouver Sun,* 27 October 1995.
119 Mark Mosley, "Welcome to the Republic of Pacifica," *Vancouver Sun,* 7 March 1991.
120 Cited by Gordon Gibson, "BC Separatism Is No Joke, M. Chretien," *Vancouver Sun,* 10 May 1994.
121 Daphne Bramham, "Breaking Away: The Case for Independence," *Vancouver Sun,* 27 October 1995, A4.
122 Gordon Wilson, *A Civilized Revolution* (Vancouver: Ronsdale Press, 1996), 107.
123 Mair, *Canada: Is Anyone Listening?* 158, 233.
124 Neale Adams, "Portrait of a Province in Its Life of Independence," *Vancouver Sun,* 12 March 1977.
125 David Beers, "Vancouver Secedes: Birth of a Nation," *Vancouver Magazine,* October 1997.
126 Marian Bruce, "Northern Vancouver Island Threatens to Join Alaska," *Vancouver Sun,* 6 November 1974.
127 Cited by Gary Mason, *Vancouver Sun,* 22 June 1989.
128 Robert White-Harvey, "Why Vancouver Island Should Go It Alone," *Globe and Mail,* 14 March 1998, D9.
129 Marjorie Nichols, *Vancouver Sun,* 19 March 1980.
130 Marjorie Nichols, "Greed Addles the Socred Brains," *Vancouver Sun,* 22 July 1980.
131 Marjorie Nichols, *Vancouver Sun,* 28 November 1980.
132 Cited in *Vancouver Sun,* 24 November 1980.
133 *Vancouver Sun,* 16 February 1977.
134 Allan Fotheringham, *Vancouver Sun,* 1 March 1980.
135 Denny Boyd, *Vancouver Sun,* 16 April 1981.
136 Tom Berger, "English Canada and Quebec's Rendezvous with Independence," 2.
137 Cited in Cernetig, "Yin and Yang of BC Nationalism," D1.
138 Cited in Daphne Bramham, "Breaking Away: The Cost of Nationhood," *Vancouver Sun,* 28 October 1995, A4.
139 Peter McMartin, "Carney an Intelligent, Dedicated Woman – but She Has to Be Stopped," *Vancouver Sun,* 30 September 1997, B1.
140 Barbara Yaffe, "BC's Own Father of (De)Confederation. Gordon Wilson's Canada Would Be a Decentralized Country. Which Is How He Came to Share a Platform with Secessionists," *Vancouver Sun,* 11 February 1998, A15.
141 Gibson, "BC Separatism Is No Joke, M. Chretien."
142 Pierre Trudeau, cited in Michael Valpy, *Vancouver Sun,* 4 November 1980.
143 Editorial, *Vancouver Sun,* 27 September 1997.
144 For a brief discussion of the five-region concept, see David Mitchell, "BC's Biggest Constitutional Contribution? A Canada of Five Regions," *Vancouver Sun,* 19 December 1997.
145 Smith, *Renewal of the Federation,* 40.
146 Ibid., 95.
147 Mair, *Canada: Is Anyone Listening?* 75, 131.
148 Ibid., 232.
149 Jerry Collins, "How to Answer a 'Yes' Vote. Gordon Gibson's Guidebook to Post-Quebec Canada," *British Columbia Report,* 4 July 1994, 11-12, on Gordon Gibson's book *Plan B: The Future of the Rest of Canada.*
150 Vancouver Board of Trade, "Future of the Federation," 27.
151 Business Council of BC, "The Future of Canada," 10.

152 Berger, "English Canada and Quebec's Rendezvous," 2, 5.

153 Burns, "The Course of True Love," 11, 14.

154 Clark, "With Our Nation in Peril," 23.

155 BC Teachers' Federation, "National Unity," Brief to the BC Unity Panel, December 1997, 3, 4.

156 Edward McWhinney, "Constitution-Making for an Era of Transition," in *Discussion Papers on British Columbia in Confederation* (Victoria: Queen's Printer for British Columbia, 1991), 68.

157 "BC Has Embraced the Larger World All Canada Seeks," *Vancouver Sun*, 28 October 1995, A22.

158 David Mitchell, "BC Is Showing Signs of Emerging from Its Splendid Isolation and Wanting to Play a Part in Debates About the Future of Confederation," *Vancouver Sun*, 14 October 1997.

159 Barman, *The West beyond the West*, 361, 362.

160 Cited in Barbara Yaffe, "Clark Shows Little Leadership on the Issue of Canadian Unity," *Vancouver Sun*, 24 June 1997, A3.

161 Enemark, "Constitutional Reform," 33-4.

162 *Vancouver Sun*, 24 January 1981.

163 Patrick Nagle, "Drop Petty Gripes, Trudeau Tells BC," *Vancouver Sun*, 25 November 1981.

164 Carol Volkart, "Out of Touch? BC Answers Trudeau," *Vancouver Sun*, 26 November 1981.

Chapter 4: BC Public Opinion and Canadian Unity

1 BC Unity Panel, *Report on the Calgary Declaration* (Vancouver, 1998), 6-7.

2 Ibid., 9-10.

3 Ibid., Telephone Survey Appendix, 3.

4 Ibid., 13-4.

5 Ibid., 17.

6 Ibid., 20; Appendix, 6.

7 Ibid., 21-2.

8 Ibid., 23.

9 Ibid., 24-5.

10 Ibid., 26.

11 Ibid., 28-9.

12 Ibid., 5.

13 All the collocates shown in Figure 2 appear in at least ten different sentences where the term *Quebec* occurs, and all associations are statistically significant at 99.9%.

14 BC Unity Talks, *Appendices: Report on the Calgary Declaration,* 12 February 1998, 4. The focus groups were held during the first week of December 1997 in six BC communities: Vancouver, Surrey, Kelowna, Terrace, Campbell River, and Prince George. There were two sessions per community.

15 All quotations presented in this form come from briefs that were submitted to the BC Unity Panel in November and December 1997 and that are in the files compiled by the Unity Panel. To protect the identities of the writers, only initials and places of residence are shown here.

16 This quotation is taken from the focus groups: BC Unity Talks, *Appendices*, 22.

17 This and the previous quotation are taken from the focus groups: ibid., 8

18 Ibid.
19 This and the previous quotation are taken from the focus groups: ibid., 17-8.

Chapter 5: A Region-Province?

1 Robin Fisher, "*BC Studies* and British Columbia History," *BC Studies* (Winter 1993-94), 76.
2 Michael Keating, *The New Regionalism in Western Europe: Territorial Restructuring and Political Change* (Cheltenham, UK: Edward Elgar, 1998), 10.
3 Ibid., 90-92.
4 Kenichi Ohmae, *The End of the Nation State: The Rise of Regional Economies* (New York: Free Press, 1995), 7, 79.
5 Colin Williams, "Territory, Identity and Language," in *The Political Economy of Regionalism,* ed. Michael Keating and John Loughlin (London: Frank Cass, 1997), 119.
6 Thomas J. Courchene with Colin Telmer, *From Heartland to North American Region State: The Social, Fiscal and Federal Evolution of Ontario,* Faculty of Management, University of Toronto, Monograph Series on Public Policy (Toronto, 1998), 10.
7 Ohmae, *End of the Nation State,* 80.
8 Ibid., 100.
9 Williams, "Territory, Identity and Language," 119.
10 Ernest Renan, *Qu'est-ce qu'une nation?* (1882; reprint Paris: Agora, 1992). An English translation of the passage quoted above is provided in John Hutchinson and Anthony D. Smith, eds., *Nationalism* (Oxford: Oxford University Press, 1994), 17.
11 Of the many works that analyze the nature of the modern state, I would refer to the collection edited by Ali Kazancigil, *The State in Global Perspective* (Aldershot, UK: UNESCO/Gower, 1986).
12 John F. Helliwell and John McCallum, "National Borders Still Matter for Trade," *Policy Options* (July-August 1995): 45. To be fair to Courchene, the figures for Canada-US trade have expanded considerably in the 1990s, while the trade data that form the basis for the Helliwell and McCallum calculations go back to the first year of operation of the Canada-US Free Trade Agreement, 1989. As William Watson has argued, however, "even if our 'overtrading' with ourselves is eroded by the FTA, the erosion will have to be huge in order to eliminate it altogether. Cut east-west trade in half – or double north-south trade – and Canadians will still be trading with each other ten times more than they would if the border didn't matter" (*Globalization and the Meaning of Canadian Life* [Toronto: University of Toronto Press, 1998], 53).
13 Renan, *Qu'est-ce qu'une nation?,* 17.
14 Liah Greenfeld, *Nationalism: Five Roads to Modernity* (Cambridge, MA: Harvard University Press, 1992), 15-6.
15 See Charles Taylor, *Reconciling the Solitudes* (Montreal: McGill-Queen's University Press, 1993), especially Chapters 3 and 8; also *The Politics of Recognition* (Princeton, NJ: Princeton University Press, 1992).
16 On the subject of constitutional politics, see Alan Cairns, *Disruptions: Constitutional Struggle from the Charter to Meech Lake* (Toronto: McClelland and Stewart, 1991); Peter Russell, *Constitutional Odyssey: Can Canadians be a Sovereign People?* (Toronto: University of Toronto Press, 1992); Alan Cairns,

"Constitutional Reform: The God that Failed," in *Transactions of the Royal Society of Canada, Can Canada Survive?* (Toronto: University of Toronto Press, 1997), 47-66.

17 Constitution du Royaume d'Espagne (1978) in Henri Oberdorff, ed., *Les constitutions de l'Europe des Douze* (Paris: La documentation française, 1994), 109 (my translation).

18 Rafe Mair, *Canada: Is Anyone Listening?* 231-2. See also some of the statements by ordinary British Columbians cited in Chapter 4.

19 See Ramsay Cook, ed., *French Canadian Nationalism* (Toronto: Macmillan, 1969); Kenneth McRoberts, "The First Century: Separate Nationalities," chap. 1 in *Misconceiving Canada: The Struggle for National Unity* (Toronto: Oxford University Press, 1997).

20 See the series in *Le Devoir*, edited by Jean Pichette and Michel Venne, entitled *Penser la nation québécoise: Comment vivre ensemble?* that ran from 19 June through 4 September 1999. This has since been published in a book.

21 Keating, *The New Regionalism in Western Europe*, 11.

22 European Union, Committee of the Regions, *Regions and Cities, Pillars of Europe* (Amsterdam: European Union, 1997), 6.

23 Roger Gibbins, *Regionalism: Territorial Politics in Canada and the United States* (Toronto: Butterworth, 1982), 176.

Chapter 6: What If?

1 Supreme Court of Canada, *Reference Re Secession of Quebec,* 20 August 1998, 87.

2 Robert Young has done a good job of outlining the serious legitimacy crisis that would have arisen regarding the result had the "yes" side secured a narrow victory in the October 1995 referendum. 86,501 ballots, or 1.82 percent of all ballots cast, were, in fact, rejected. These rejected ballots were, however, overwhelmingly concentrated in three ridings – Chomedey, Marguerite-Bourgeoys, and Laurier-Dorion – with very large anti-sovereignty electorates. According to Young, "had there been a narrow Yes victory, every rejected ballot throughout the province would have been considered a potential No vote, and the legitimacy of the result would have been deeply contested ... Canadians would not be prepared to countenance 'letting Quebec go' by electoral fraud" (Robert Young, *The Struggle for Quebec* [Montreal: McGill-Queen's University Press, 1999], 70-1).

3 Grand Council of the Crees, *Sovereign Injustice: Forcible Inclusion of the James Bay Crees and Cree Territory in a Sovereign Quebec* (Nemaska, QC, 1995).

4 For a discussion of some of the issues that might arise regarding the debt, see Harold Chorney, "Dividing the National Debt: More than Bean Counting," in *Negotiating with a Sovereign Quebec,* ed. Daniel Drache and Roberto Perin (Toronto: Lorimer, 1992), 156-69; Alan Freeman and Patrick Grady, *Dividing the House: Planning for a Canada without Quebec* (Toronto: HarperCollins, 1995).

5 Supreme Court of Canada, *Reference Re Secession of Quebec,* 92.

6 See the argument for an ongoing shared Canada-Quebec responsibility for the Aboriginal population of Quebec, in the event of Quebec acceding to sovereignty, made by Reg Whitaker, "Sovereignties Old and New: Canada, Quebec and Aboriginal Peoples," *Studies in Political Economy* (Spring 1999): 69-96. Whether such an arrangement could in fact be negotiated is another story.

7 Premier William Bennett, Speech to the Montreal Board of Trade, 12 May 1980, 11, 13, 15.
8 Premier Mike Harcourt, cited in Patrick Nagle, "Separatists' 'global pretensions' offend BC," *Vancouver Sun*, 19 May 1994.
9 Gordon Gibson, *Thirty Million Musketeers* (Vancouver: Fraser Institute/Key Porter, 1995), 237.
10 Tom Berger, "English Canada and Quebec's Rendezvous with Independence," in *Discussion Papers on British Columbia in Confederation* (Victoria: Queen's Printer for British Columbia, 1991), 3.
11 Bloc Québécois, *Chantier de réflexion sur le partenariat*, English version, 1999, 14-5.
12 Ibid., 16.

Bibliography

Government Documents

British Columbia

British Columbia. Intergovernmental Relations Secretariat. BC Premiers and Ministers of Intergovernmental Affairs, Statements and Speeches, for the most part to Federal-Provincial Conferences, 1962-98.

British Columbia. Parliament. Legislative Debates, various years.

British Columbia in the Canadian Confederation. Submission to the Royal Commission on Dominion-Provincial Relations by the Government of British Columbia. Victoria, 1938.

British Columbia Unity Panel. *Report on the Calgary Declaration*. Vancouver, 12 February 1998.

–. Transcripts of Public Hearings of the BC Unity Panel in Chilliwack, Cranbrook, Fort St. John, Kamloops, Kelowna, Nanaimo, Prince George, Peachland, Vancouver Eastside, Vancouver Westside, and Victoria, November-December 1997.

–. Written Briefs Submitted to the BC Unity Panel, November-December 1997.

British Columbia Unity Talks. *Appendices: Report on the Calgary Declaration*. Vancouver, 12 February 1998.

Confederation for the Twenty-First Century, Discussion Papers on British Columbia in Confederation. Victoria: Queen's Printer for British Columbia, 1991. (This document includes the papers by Tom Berger, Ron Burns, R.M. Clark, Tex Enemark, Walter Hardwick, Alma Howard, Edward McWhinney, and Cyril Shelford that are listed separately under "Books and Articles" in this bibliography.)

Gibson, Gordon. *Renewing the Federation: Options for British Columbia*. Victoria: Queen's Printer for British Columbia, 1997.

Government of British Columbia. *BC Media Handbook: Your Guide to British Columbia, Gateway to the Pacific Century*. Prepared for the 1997 Asia Pacific Economic Cooperation summit conference in Vancouver. 1997.

Smith, Melvin H. *The Renewal of the Federation: A British Columbia Perspective*. Victoria: Queen's Printer for British Columbia, 1991.

Canada

Canada Year Book 1999. Ottawa, 1998.

Canadian Crime Statistics. Ottawa, 1997.

Perspectives Canada III. Ottawa: Statistics Canada, 1980.

Statistics Canada. "Breaking and Entering in Canada." *Juristat* 18, no. 5 (1996).

Supreme Court of Canada. *Reference Re Secession of Quebec,* 20 August 1998.

Selected Newspaper and Magazine Articles

Adams, Neale. "Portrait of a Province in Its Life of Independence." *Vancouver Sun,* 12 March 1977.

Baldrey, Keith. "BC Seeks Greater Economic Autonomy." *Vancouver Sun,* 9 June 1990.

Barrett, Tom. "BC Will Be the Tough Background." *Vancouver Sun,* 19 September 1992.

"BC Unimpressed by Separatism." *Globe and Mail,* 5 December 1995.

Beers, David. "Vancouver Secedes: Birth of a Nation." *Vancouver Magazine,* October 1997.

Berger, Tom. "Among Quebec's Distinctions Is Its Struggle for Its Identity." *Vancouver Sun,* 24 October 1997.

Boei, William. "Premier Has New Doubts on Meech: Vander Zalm Says He Wouldn't Sign Pact if Faced with It Again." *Vancouver Sun,* 30 June 1990, A1.

Bramham, Daphne. "Breaking Away: The Case for Independence." *Vancouver Sun,* 27 October 1995, A4.

–. "Breaking Away: The Cost of Nationhood." *Vancouver Sun,* 28 October 1995, A4.

Bruce, Marian. "Northern Vancouver Island Threatens to Join Alaska." *Vancouver Sun,* 6 November 1974.

Byfield, Ted. "Why Can't the Rest of Us Put Limits on Quebec's Referendum Habit?" *British Columbia Report,* 12 September 1994, 44.

Cernetig, Miro. "Blue Grit." *Globe and Mail Report on Business Magazine,* April 1996, 75-88.

–. "The Yin and Yang of BC Nationalism." *Globe and Mail,* 27 September 1997, D1-2.

Collins, Jerry. "How to Answer a 'Yes' Vote. Gordon Gibson's Guidebook to Post-Quebec Canada." *British Columbia Report,* 4 July 1994, 11-2.

Coupland, Douglas. "Vancouver: Our Future." *Vancouver Magazine,* October 1997, 52.

Deacon, James. "Green Cathedrals: BC Tourism Enjoys a Backcountry Boom." *Maclean's,* 24 August 1992.

Doyle, Kevin. "Where the Sun Shines Best." *Maclean's,* 24 August 1992, 4.

Editorials. *Vancouver Sun,* 1934-99.

Farrow, Moira. "Provincial Governments Are the Villains." *Vancouver Sun,* 30 June 1980.

Fennell, Tom, and Frances Kelly. "The Right Stuff?" *Maclean's,* 24 August 1992.

Fotheringham, Allan. "Smelling Flowers in the Slow Lane." *Maclean's,* 24 August 1992, 64.

Fulford, Robert. "Dream Country." *Vancouver Sun,* 14 January 1976.

Gibson, Gordon. "BC Separatism Is No Joke, M. Chretien." *Vancouver Sun,* 10 May 1994.

Gill, Ian. "A Green Island in a Sea of Envy: Welcome to Cascadia." *Georgia Straight,* 5-12 June 1992, 7-9.

Goar, Carol. "Some Bargainers Did a Bit Better than Others. Mike Harcourt, Unfortunately, Wasn't Among Them." *Vancouver Sun,* 25 August 1992, A11.

Greenspon, Edward, and Graham Fraser. "PM Finds More Cash to Woo Provinces: On Eve of Talks with Premiers, He Prepares to Sweeten Health Offer." *Globe and Mail,* 3 February 1999, A1.

Gwyn, Richard. "West's Alienation Growing into Separatism." *Vancouver Sun,* 19 February 1977.

Hayes, Charles. "The Henpecked Revolutionary. Secede, Says the Okanagan's Fred Washburn." *British Columbia Report,* 26 February 1990, 44.

Hobbs, Lisa Birnie. "The West Coast: A Unique Land with a Powerful Sense of Newness." *Vancouver Sun,* 10 August 1996, A19.

Hunter, Justine. "BC Gets Short End of the Stick from Ottawa." *Vancouver Sun,* 9 December 1995, A18.

Hutchison, Bruce. Various articles. *Vancouver Sun,* 1980-90.

Koch, George. "Confederation in Crisis." *British Columbia Report,* 29 January 1990, 15-7.

McGeer, Pat. "Standing Behind Regional Strength." *Vancouver Sun,* 23 May 1990, A13.

McMartin, Peter. "Carney an Intelligent, Dedicated Woman – but She Has to Be Stopped." *Vancouver Sun,* 30 September 1997, B1.

Meisler, Stanley. "Us, as Seen by One of Them: An American's Look at BC." *Vancouver Sun,* 15 May 1980.

Mitchell, David. Various articles. *Vancouver Sun,* 1995-97.

Mosley, Mark. "Welcome to the Republic of Pacifica." *Vancouver Sun,* 7 March 1991.

Mulgrew, Ian. "Angry Carney Says BC Shouldn't Rule Out Separation." *Vancouver Sun,* 25 September 1997.

Nagle, Patrick. "Drop Petty Gripes, Trudeau Tells BC." *Vancouver Sun,* 25 November 1981.

Newman, Peter. "Essay." *Maclean's,* 24 August 1992, 13.

Nichols, Marjorie. "Greed Addles the Socred Brains." *Vancouver Sun,* 22 July 1980.

O'Neil, Peter. Various articles. *Vancouver Sun,* 1992-98.

Owen, Robert. "Faultlines of the New Europe: Fragile States in Danger of Destruction." *The Times* (London), 29 December 1998.

Palmer, Vaughn. Various articles. *Vancouver Sun,* 1989-97.

Pichette, Jean, and Michel Venne, eds. *Penser la nation québécoise: Comment vivre ensemble?* 12-part series of articles, *Le Devoir,* Summer 1999.

Rinehart, Diane. "BC Boom Tops National Census." *Vancouver Sun,* 16 April 1997.

Russell, Frances. "Victoria's Shameful Separatism Show." *Vancouver Sun,* 24 January 1977.

Sutherland, Jim. "Poll: Viewpoints Research Asked 700 of You Some Very Intimate Questions. Here Are Your Answers." *Vancouver Magazine,* December 1998, 55-69.

Todd, Douglas. "Poll Finds BC Least Religious." *Vancouver Sun,* 29 November 1996.

Volkart, Carol. "Out of Touch? BC Answers Trudeau." *Vancouver Sun,* 26 November 1981.

Ward, Doug. "Vander Zalm Steps into Meech Lake Fray." *Vancouver Sun,* 18 January 1990.

White-Harvey, Robert. "Why Vancouver Island Should Go It Alone." *Globe and Mail,* 14 March 1998, D9.

Yaffe, Barbara. Various articles. *Vancouver Sun,* 1994-98.

Books and Articles

Anderson, Benedict. *Imagined Communities: Reflections on the Origin and Spread of Nationalism.* Rev. ed. London: Verso, 1991.

Barman, Jean. *The West beyond the West: A History of British Columbia.* Rev. ed. Toronto: University of Toronto Press, 1996.

Barnes, T., D. Edgington, K. Denike, and T. McGee. "Vancouver, the Province, and the Pacific Rim." In *Vancouver and Its Region,* edited by Graeme Wynn and Timothy Oke, 171-99. Vancouver: UBC Press, 1992.

Bateman, Rebecca. "Comparative Thoughts on the Politics of Aboriginal Assimilation." *BC Studies* 114 (Summer 1997): 59-83.

Bell, David. *The Roots of Disunity: A Study of Canadian Political Culture.* Rev. ed. Toronto: Oxford University Press, 1992.

Belshaw, Cyril. In *Transactions of the Thirteenth BC Natural Resources Conference, 1961,* 323-7.

Berger, Tom. "English Canada and Quebec's Rendezvous with Independence." In *Discussion Papers on British Columbia in Confederation,* 1-6. Victoria: Queen's Printer for British Columbia, 1991.

Birney, Earle. *The Collected Poems of Earle Birney.* Toronto: McClelland and Stewart, 1975.

Black, Edwin R. "British Columbia: The Politics of Exploitation." In *Party Politics in Canada,* 4th ed., edited by Hugh Thorburn. Scarborough, ON: Prentice Hall, 1979.

Blake, Don, Neil Guppy, and Peter Urmetzer. "Being Green in BC: Public Attitudes Towards Environmental Issues." *BC Studies* (Winter 1996-97): 41-61.

Bloc Québécois. *Chantier de réflexion sur le partenariat,* English version, 1999.

Bobbio, Norberto. *Left and Right: The Significance of a Political Distinction.* Chicago: University of Chicago Press, 1996.

Brown, Justine. "Nowherelands: Utopian Communities in BC Fiction." *BC Studies* (Spring 1996): 5-28.

Burns, Ron. "The Course of True Love Never Did Run Smooth." In *Discussion Papers on British Columbia in Confederation,* 7-14. Victoria: Queen's Printer for British Columbia, 1991.

Cairns, Alan. "Socialism, Federalism, and the BC Party System." In *Party Politics in Canada,* 5th ed., edited by Hugh Thorburn. Toronto: Prentice Hall, 1985.

–. "The Governments and Societies of Canadian Federalism." In *Constitution, Government, and Society in Canada: Selected Essays.* Toronto: McClelland and Stewart, 1988.

–. *Disruptions: Constitutional Struggle from the Charter to Meech Lake.* Toronto: McClelland and Stewart, 1991.

–. "Constitutional Reform: The God that Failed." In *Transactions of the Royal Society of Canada, Can Canada Survive?* 47-66. Toronto: University of Toronto Press, 1997.

Careless, J.M.S. "Limited Identities in Canada." *Canadian Historical Review* 50 (1969): 1-10.

Cernetig, Miro. "The Far Side of the Rockies: Politics and Identity in British Columbia." In *A Passion for Identity,* edited by David Taras and Beverley Rasporich, 449-62. Toronto: Nelson, 1997.

Chorney, Harold. "Dividing the National Debt: More than Bean Counting." In *Negotiating with a Sovereign Quebec,* edited by Daniel Drache and Roberto Perin, 156-69. Toronto: Lorimer, 1992.

Citizens' Forum on Canada's Future. Ottawa: Minister of Supply and Services, 1991.

Clark, Robert. "With Our Nation in Peril, What Should British Columbia Do?" In *Discussion Papers on British Columbia in Confederation,* 15-28. Victoria: Queen's Printer for British Columbia, 1991.

Cook, Ramsay, ed. *French Canadian Nationalism.* Toronto: Macmillan, 1969.

Coupland, Douglas. *Life after God.* New York: Pocketbooks, 1994.

Courchene, Thomas J., with Colin Telmer. *From Heartland to North American Region State: The Social, Fiscal and Federal Evolution of Ontario.* Faculty of Management, University of Toronto, Monograph Series on Public Policy. Toronto, 1998.

Economic Council of Canada. *Living Together: A Study of Regional Disparities.* Ottawa, 1977.

Editorial. *BC Studies* (Autumn/Winter 1997-98): 3-6.

Elkins, David. "British Columbia as a State of Mind." In *Two Political Worlds,* Donald Blake. Vancouver: UBC Press, 1985.

–. "Politics as a Canadian Game." *BC Studies* (Winter 1993-94): 43-58.

Elshtain, Jean Bethke. *Democracy on Trial.* Concord, ON: Anansi, 1993.

Elton, David. "Federalism and the Canadian West." In *Perspectives on Canadian Federalism,* edited by R.D. Olling and M.M. Westmacott. Scarborough, ON: Prentice Hall, 1988.

Employers' Council of British Columbia. *Populism, Partisanship, and Progress.* Vancouver, November 1978.

Enemark, Tex. "Constitutional Reform: A Radical BC Proposal." In *Discussion Papers on British Columbia in Confederation,* 29-41. Victoria: Queen's Printer for British Columbia, 1991.

European Union. Committee of the Regions. *Regions and Cities, Pillars of Europe.* Amsterdam, 1997.

Fisher, Robin. *Duff Pattullo of British Columbia.* Toronto: University of Toronto Press, 1991.

–. *"BC Studies* and British Columbia History." *BC Studies* (Winter 1993-94): 59-77.

Freeman, Alan, and Patrick Grady. *Dividing the House: Planning for a Canada without Quebec.* Toronto: HarperCollins, 1995.

Friesen, Gerald. *The West: Regional Ambitions, National Debates, Global Age.* Toronto: Penguin, 1999.

Galbraith, Gordon S. "British Columbia." In *The Provincial Political Systems,* edited by David Bellamy et al., 62-75. Toronto: Methuen, 1971.

Garr, Allen. *Tough Guy: Bill Bennett and the Taking of British Columbia*. Toronto: Key Porter, 1985.

Garreau, Joel. *The Nine Nations of North America*. Boston: Houghton Mifflin, 1981.

Gawthrop, Daniel. *Highwire Act: Power, Pragmatism, and the Harcourt Legacy.* Vancouver: New Star Books, 1996.

Gellner, Ernest. *Nationalism*. London: Weidenfeld and Nicolson, 1997.

Gibbins, Roger. *Regionalism: Territorial Politics in Canada and the United States*. Toronto: Butterworth, 1982.

Gibbins, Roger, and Sonia Arrison. *Western Visions: Perspectives on the West in Canada*. Peterborough, ON: Broadview Press, 1995.

Gibson, Gordon. *Thirty Million Musketeers*. Vancouver: Fraser Institute/Key Porter, 1995.

–. "A Principled Analysis of the Nisga'a Treaty." *Inroads* no. 8 (1999): 163-78.

Grand Council of the Crees. *Sovereign Injustice: Forcible Inclusion of the James Bay Crees and Cree Territory in a Sovereign Quebec*. Nemaska, QC, 1995.

Greenfeld, Liah. *Nationalism: Five Roads to Modernity*. Cambridge, MA: Harvard University Press, 1992.

Haig-Brown, Roderick. "British Columbia: Loggers and Lotus Eaters." In *Canada: A Guide to the Peaceable Kingdom,* edited by William Kilbourn, 124-8. Toronto: Macmillan, 1970.

Halpenny, Frances. "The Humanities in Canada: A Study of Structure." In *Re-Inventing the Humanities: International Perspectives,* edited by David Myers, 155-65. Kew: Australian Scholarly Publishers, 1995.

Harcourt, Mike, and Wayne Skene. *Harcourt: A Measure of Defiance*. Vancouver: Douglas and McIntyre, 1996.

Hardwick, Walter. "Re-ordering Canada." In *Discussion Papers on British Columbia in Confederation,* 50-5. Victoria: Queen's Printer for British Columbia, 1991.

Harris, Cole. *The Resettlement of British Columbia*. Vancouver: UBC Press, 1997.

Helliwell, John F., and John McCallum. "National Borders Still Matter for Trade." *Policy Options* (July-August 1995): 44-8.

Hobsbawm, Eric, and Terence Ranger, eds. *The Invention of Tradition*. Cambridge: Cambridge University Press, 1983.

Hodgins, Jack, ed. *The West Coast Experience*. Toronto: Macmillan, 1976.

Howard, Alma. "British Columbia and Canada's Future." In *Discussion Papers on British Columbia in Confederation,* 56-63. Victoria: Queen's Printer for British Columbia, 1991.

Hutchison, Bruce. *The Fraser*. Toronto: Clarke, Irwin, 1950.

–. "Surrender of Separatism." In *British Columbia: A Centennial Anthology,* edited by Reginald E. Watters, 455-6. Toronto: McClelland and Stewart, 1958.

Hutton, Thomas A. *The Transformation of Canada's Pacific Metropolis: A Study of Vancouver.* Montreal: Institute for Research on Public Policy, 1998.

Jamieson, Stuart. *Times of Trouble: Labour Unrest and Industrial Conflict in Canada, 1900-1966*. Task Force on Labour Relations, Study 22. Ottawa, 1966.

Kazancigil, Ali, ed. *The State in Global Perspective*. Aldershot, UK: UNESCO/Gower, 1986.

Keating, Michael. *The New Regionalism in Western Europe: Territorial Restructuring and Political Change*. Cheltenham, UK: Edward Elgar, 1998.

Keene, Roger, and David Humphreys, eds. *Conversations with W.A.C. Bennett.* Toronto: Methuen, 1980.

Kilgour, David. *Inside Outer Canada.* Edmonton: Lone Pine, 1990.

Lipset, Seymour Martin. *Continental Divide.* London: Routledge, 1990.

Magnusson, Warren, et al., eds. *The New Reality.* Vancouver: New Star Books, 1984.

Mair, Rafe. *Canada: Is Anyone Listening?* Toronto: Key Porter, 1998.

Mason, Gary, and Keith Baldrey. *Fantasyland: Inside the Reign of Bill Vander Zalm.* Toronto: McGraw-Hill Ryerson, 1989.

McIsaac, Ron, and Anne Champagne, eds. *Clayoquot Mass Trials: Defending the Rainforest.* Gabriola, BC: New Society Publishers, 1994.

McRoberts, Kenneth. *Misconceiving Canada: The Struggle for National Unity.* Toronto: Oxford University Press, 1997.

McWhinney, Edward. "Constitution-Making for an Era of Transition." In *Discussion Papers on British Columbia in Confederation,* 64-71. Victoria: Queen's Printer for British Columbia, 1991.

Métin, Albert. *La Colombie-Britannique.* Paris: Armand Colin, 1908.

Mitchell, David J. *WAC: Bennett and the Rise of British Columbia.* Vancouver: Douglas and McIntyre, 1983.

Oberdorff, Henri, ed. *Les constitutions de l'Europe des Douze.* Paris: La documentation française, 1994.

Odum, Howard, and Harry Moore, eds. *American Regionalism: A Cultural-Historical Approach to National Integration.* New York: Henry Holt, 1938.

Ohmae, Kenichi. *The End of the Nation State: The Rise of Regional Economies.* New York: Free Press, 1995.

Ormsby, Margaret. *British Columbia: A History.* Toronto: Macmillan, 1958.

Ornstein, Michael. "Regionalism and Canadian Political Ideology." In *Regionalism in Canada,* edited by Richard Brym. Toronto: Clarke, Irwin, 1986.

Prang, Margaret, and John Norris, eds. *Personality and History in British Columbia: Essays in Honour of Margaret Ormsby.* Vancouver: BC Studies, 1977.

Pethick, Derek. "The Confederation Debate of 1870." In *British Columbia and Confederation,* edited by George Shelton. Victoria: Morriss Printing, 1967.

Pinard, Maurice, Robert Bernier, and Vincent Lemieux. *Un combat inachevé.* Saint Foy: Presses de l'Université du Québec, 1997.

Rawlyk, George A., Bruce Hodgins, and Richard Bowles, eds. *Regionalism in Canada: Flexible Federalism or Fractured Nation?* Scarborough, ON: Prentice Hall, 1979.

Renan, Ernest. *Qu'est-ce qu'une nation?* 1882. Reprint, Paris: Agora, 1992 (excerpted in John Hutchinson and Anthony D. Smith, eds., *Nationalism* [Oxford: Oxford University Press, 1994], 16-7).

Resnick, Philip. "BC Capitalism and the Empire of the Pacific." *BC Studies* (Autumn 1985): 29-46.

–. "Neo-Conservatism on the Periphery: The Lessons from British Columbia." *BC Studies* (Autumn 1987): 7-23.

–. "Whatever Happened to Civil Society?" In *Twenty-First Century Democracy,* chap. 7. Montreal: McGill-Queen's University Press, 1997.

–. "West Coast Blues. Why BC? Why PC?" *Inroads,* no. 8 (1999): 179-91.

Ricou, Laurie. "The Writing of British Columbia Writing." *BC Studies* (Winter 1993-94): 106-20.

Robin, Martin. *The Rush to Spoils: The Company Province 1871-1933*. Toronto: McClelland and Stewart, 1972.

Robinson, J. Lewis, and W.G. Hardwick. "The Canadian Cordillera." In *Canada: A Geographical Interpretation,* edited by John Warkentin, 438-72. Toronto: Methuen, 1968.

Ruff, Norman. "British Columbia and Canadian Federalism." In *The Reins of Power: Governing British Columbia,* edited by Terence Morley et al. Vancouver: Douglas and McIntyre, 1983.

–. "Pacific Perspectives on the Canadian Confederation." In *Canada: The State of the Federation 1991,* edited by Douglas M. Brown. Kingston, ON: Queen's University, Institute for Intergovernmental Relations, 1991.

Russell, Peter. *Constitutional Odyssey: Can Canadians Be a Sovereign People?* Toronto: University of Toronto Press, 1992.

Ryan, Claude. "The Agreement on the Canadian Social Union as Seen by a Quebec Federalist." *Inroads,* no. 8 (1999): 25-41.

Shearer, Ronald. "The Economy." *BC Studies* (Winter 1993-94): 121-39.

Shelford, Cyril. "Canada's Future." In *Discussion Papers on British Columbia in Confederation,* 77-9. Victoria: Queen's Printer for British Columbia, 1991.

Sherman, Paddy. *Bennett.* Toronto: McClelland and Stewart, 1966.

Skelton, Robin. "Night Poem, Vancouver Island." In *Contemporary Poetry of British Columbia,* edited by Michael Yates, 1. Victoria: Sono Nis, 1970.

–, ed. *Six Poets of British Columbia.* Victoria: Sono Nis Press, 1980.

Smiley, Donald. *Canada in Question: Federalism in the Seventies.* Toronto: McGraw-Hill Ryerson, 1976.

Smith, Allan. *Canada: An American Nation?* Montreal: McGill-Queen's University Press, 1994.

Stevenson, Garth. *Ex Uno Plures.* Montreal: McGill-Queen's University Press, 1993.

Taylor, Charles. *The Malaise of Modernity.* Concord, ON: Anansi, 1991.

–. *The Politics of Recognition.* Princeton, NJ: Princeton University Press, 1992.

–. *Reconciling the Solitudes.* Montreal: McGill-Queen's University Press, 1993.

Tennant, Paul. "Aboriginal Peoples and Aboriginal Title in British Columbia Politics." In *Politics, Policy, and Government in British Columbia,* edited by R.K. Carty, 45-64. Vancouver: UBC Press, 1996.

Tippett, Maria, and Douglas Cole. *From Desolation to Splendour: Changing Perceptions of the British Columbia Landscape.* Toronto: Clarke, Irwin, 1977.

Tomblin, Stephen. *Ottawa and the Outer Provinces: The Challenge of Regional Integration in Canada.* Toronto: Lorimer, 1995.

Tully, James. *Strange Multiplicity: Constitutionalism in an Age of Diversity.* Cambridge: Cambridge University Press, 1995.

Twigg, Alan. *Vander Zalm: From Immigrant to Premier.* Madeira Park, BC: Harbour Publishing, 1986.

Urquhart, M.C., and K.A.M. Buckley, eds. *Historical Statistics of Canada.* Toronto: Macmillan, 1965.

Ward, Peter. *White Canada Forever: Popular Attitudes and Public Policy toward Orientals in British Columbia.* Montreal: McGill-Queen's University Press, 1978.

Watson, William. *Globalization and the Meaning of Canadian Life.* Toronto: University of Toronto Press, 1998.

Whitaker, Reg. "Sovereignties Old and New: Canada, Quebec and Aboriginal Peoples." *Studies in Political Economy* (Spring 1999): 69-96.

Williams, Colin. "Territory, Identity and Language." In *The Political Economy of Regionalism,* edited by Michael Keating and John Loughlin. London: Frank Cass, 1997.

Wilson, Gordon. *A Civilized Revolution.* Vancouver: Ronsdale Press, 1996.

de Winter, Lieven, and Huti Tusan, eds. *Regionalist Parties in Western Europe.* London: Routledge, 1998.

Wirth, Louis. "Limitations of Regionalism." In *Regionalism in America,* edited by Merrill Jensen. Madison: University of Wisconsin Press, 1951.

Woodcock, George. *Confederation Betrayed: The Case against Trudeau's Canada.* Madeira Park, BC: Harbour Publishing, 1981.

–. *British Columbia: A History of the Province.* Vancouver: Douglas and McIntyre, 1990.

Wolfe, David. "The Emergence of the Region State." In *The Nation State in a Global/Information Era: Policy Challenges,* edited by Thomas J. Courchene, 205-40. Kingston, ON: Queen's University, John Deutsch Institute for the Study of Economic Policy, 1997.

Wrinkle, Ted. *British Columbia: BC Photographs.* Portland, OR: Beautiful West Publishing, 1977.

Young, Robert. *The Struggle for Quebec.* Montreal: McGill-Queen's University Press, 1999.

Unpublished Papers, Briefs, and Theses

Andrews, Craig Donald. "BC: A Study of the Themes of Hardship and a Sterile Land upon Its Literature, both Descriptive and Historical, 1628-1914." MA thesis, Washington State University, 1968.

British Columbia Teachers' Federation. "National Unity." Brief to the BC Unity Panel, December 1997.

Business Council of British Columbia. "The Future of Canada: A BC Business Perspective." 13 February 1992.

Canadian Jewish Congress, Pacific Region. Brief to the BC Unity Panel, 23 December 1997.

Hunt, Peter Robert. "The Political Career of Sir Richard McBride." MA thesis, University of British Columbia, 1953.

Public Service Alliance of Canada. Brief to the BC Unity Panel, December 1997.

Sanford, Thomas M. "The Politics of Protest: The CCF and Social Credit League in British Columbia." PhD thesis, University of California, Berkeley, 1961.

Vancouver Board of Trade. "Future of the Federation and Unity of Canada." Discussion paper. 5 March 1997.

Index